Assessing Student Threats

A Handbook for Implementing the Salem-Keizer System

Edited by
John Van Dreal

ROWMAN & LITTLEFIELD EDUCATION
A division of
ROWMAN & LITTLEFIELD PUBLISHERS, INC.
Lanham • New York • Toronto • Plymouth, UK

Published by Rowman & Littlefield Education
A division of Rowman & Littlefield Publishers, Inc.
A wholly owned subsidiary of The Rowman & Littlefield Publishing Group, Inc.
4501 Forbes Boulevard, Suite 200, Lanham, Maryland 20706
http://www.rowmaneducation.com

Estover Road, Plymouth PL6 7PY, United Kingdom

British Library Cataloguing in Publication Information Available

Library of Congress Cataloging-in-Publication Data

Van Dreal, John, 1962-
  Assessing student threats : a handbook for implementing the Salem-Keizer system / John Van Dreal.
     p. cm.
  Includes bibliographical references and index.
  ISBN 978-1-61048-110-6 (cloth : alk. paper)—ISBN 978-1-61048-111-3 (pbk. : alk. paper)—ISBN 978-1-61048-112-0 (electronic)
  1. Schools—Security measures. 2. Risk assessment 3. School violence. I. Title.
LB2866.V36 2011
363.11'9371—dc22

                                                                      2010052488

♾™ The paper used in this publication meets the minimum requirements of American National Standard for Information Sciences—Permanence of Paper for Printed Library Materials, ANSI/NISO Z39.48-1992. Printed in the United States of America

Dedicated to
those who teach,
those who administer,
those who enforce,
and
those who counsel.

Contents

Acknowledgments

As the editor and principal author I'd like to thank the following for their exceptional work in the field of threat assessment and their assistance in writing this manual (their authorship is noted by chapter in the table of contents): Rod Swinehart, Dave Okada, Allan Rainwater, Darling Mendoza, Ray Byrd, Seth Elliott, Martin Speckmaier, and Shelley Spady.

The system outlined in this manual incorporates the ideas of research experts with the application steps of practitioners. Many of the concepts presented have evolved through the examination and refinement of more than one expert and thus are the intellectual product of many. Where authorship is clear, citations are given. Where information has become generalized to the field of practice, references to the original source may have been missed, and so apologies are offered.

This author and those noted above are practitioners, not researchers. We work together daily exercising the concepts promoted in this text. As practitioners, we offer our gratitude to the following experts for their work in threat assessment. As authors, we appreciatively note their research and academic contributions. Without their leadership, our work would not be possible. They are Robert A. Fein, William Modzeleski, Mary Ellen O'Toole, J. Reid Malloy, Kris Mohandie, Eric Johnson, Gavin de Becker, Dave Grossman, Bob Martin, Randy Borum, Bryan Vossekuil, Frederick S. Calhoun, Marisa R. Randazzo, Katherine S. Newman, Andre Simons, and James Cawood.

The work done to complete this manual and formalize the above-noted threat assessment research into a functional system was only possible through the generous leadership and support of the Salem-Keizer School District in Salem, Oregon; however, the busywork of implementation and refinement is the result of the collaborative participation and efforts of the following agencies: Salem-Keizer School District, Willamette Educational Services District,

Marion County Sheriff's Office, Salem Police Department, Keizer Police Department, Oregon Judicial Department, Marion County Psychiatric Crisis Center, Polk County Children's Mental Health, Marion County Juvenile Department, Polk County Juvenile Department, Oregon Youth Authority, Marion County District Attorney's Office, Chemeketa Community College, Willamette University, and Mid-Valley Behavioral Care Network.

The following people, while not a part of this manual's authorship, have contributed ideas and/or support to the system as it has evolved: Paul Keller, Rhonda Stueve, Ruth Gelbrich, Rich Goward, Sandy Husk, Mary Paulson, Shirley Swank, Richard Swank, Raul Ramirez, David McMullen, Clem Spenner, Becky Carpenter, Michael Cunningham, Walt Myers, Marc Adams, Vicki Nishioka, Jerry Moore, Cindy Poore, Mark Whittier, Pete Teller, Coleen Van Dreal, Richard Horner, Debra Baker, Steve Kuhn, Bob Hammond, Geoff Heatherington, Linda Bonnem, Bill MacMorris-Adix, Mike McFetridge, John Troncoso, Steve Bellshaw, Craig Bazzi, Harold Burke-Sivers, Ann-Marie Bandfield, Cheri Lovre, and Bud Bailey.

Thank you to the following readers for their patience, generosity of time, and their recommendations for content editing: Robert A. Fein, William Modzeleski, Andre Simons, Kate Schoeneman, Lowell Smith, Wilson Whittaker, Jim Cawood, Eric Johnson, Owen Yardley, and Katherine S. Newman.

Finally, there are many other people who have supported the implementation of threat assessment throughout the mid-Willamette Valley and recently, throughout the Northwest...too many to mention. Hopefully they are aware of the importance of their endorsement. If not, I offer my apologies for failing to make that point and my gratitude to them for helping to make the community a safer place.

—John Van Dreal, editor and author

Disclaimer / Note Regarding the Title

The information and system outlined in this book are designed for use when assessing people who are engaged in activity or involved in circumstances that suggest the potential for aggression directed at other people. It is not designed to predict future violence nor is it a foolproof method of assessing an individual or group's risk of harm to others. It is not a strict set of risk factors or a checklist that can be quantified or added up to total a final score.

It is a guide, drawn from available research and guidelines, designed to assist in the investigation of potentially violent situations and to assist in the development and implementation of threat management plans. Finally, it is not a guide for the assessment of people who are suicidal, acting out sexually, or who are setting fires, unless they are doing so as a part of an act of aggression intending injury to others.

REGARDING THE TITLE

While the title of this book is *Assessing Student Threats: A Handbook for Implementing the Salem-Keizer System*, the system presented within the book does not actually hold that moniker. It is officially titled the Mid-Valley Student Threat Assessment System and although it is referred to locally as such, it has become known regionally and nationally as the "Salem System" or even the "Salem-Keizer System" because of its origin and location. The Salem-Keizer Public School District, located in the cities of Salem and Keizer, Oregon, was principally responsible for the development and implementation of the system at the turn of the twenty-first century. Interestingly, the word "Salem" most likely takes its origin from the Hebrew word *shalom*, meaning peace or quite possibly a similar derivation from the Hebrew word *shalem*, meaning whole or complete. *Shalom* then, because the purpose for the promotion and implementation of the system is nothing if not an earnest attempt at making our schools and communities safer and more peaceful places to live our lives. *Shalem* then, because the system outlined in this manual is certainly a wholehearted attempt at a complete and systemic approach to assessment and intervention. For all of these reasons, the title has been chosen. Well, for these reasons and possibly because the alliterative qualities of such a title were irresistible.

Information on the system is also available at http://studentthreatassessment.org.

Section 1

OVERVIEW

Chapter One

Introduction

John Van Dreal

How much more grievous are the consequences of our anger than the acts which arouse it.

—Marcus Aurelius

Marcus Aurelius knew anger. He knew how anger could lead to violence. Considered by historians to be one of Ancient Rome's most virtuous and greatest emperors, he experienced violence as one of the most successful military campaign leaders of the Imperial Expansion epoch. His observations and insight are eloquently recorded in his meditative memoirs and note the unfortunate outcome of aggressive human behavior.

The use of his words to begin this manual serves two purposes. First, to suggest that the consequences of violence perpetrated under the justification of revenge are often well beyond the act that initiates it. School shootings are the most dramatic example of this; however, one does not have to think long to identify a vindictive act, either personally experienced or observed, that confirms the lesson. And second, to note that many policies written as reactions to school and community violence are often based upon anger and fear and thus lead to ineffective, misdirected and even draconian measures.

Some school discipline code today exemplifies policy that results from a reactive and politically expedient move to address drug and alcohol use, aggressive acts, gang activity, and other delinquent behavior. Such policy tends to lead to a punitive discipline code that lumps violations into blanket generalizations and categories worthy of only one response (expulsion).

The irony is that this policy is often an attempt to make a school safer by removing students who exhibit problematic aggressive behavior without providing them with alternative education options. Such measures often increase the school's vulnerability, as those students are often less supervised and thus

3

free to move about the community and target the student body and the staff with impunity.

This manual is designed to outline a process that accurately identifies risk concerns, based upon an assessment of situational factors, and then develops supervision and intervention strategies that are fitting to those identified concerns and thus decrease risk factors. The process is neither reactive nor punitive. And while it may be employed at the same time as discipline procedures or the special education process, it is not a replacement for either. With the correct implementation of the process, schools can achieve greater safety without disruption to the normal milieu.

School violence is a significant issue because of the obvious danger involved and the fear and tension it causes for students and staff. Fear directly interferes with the higher brain functioning needed to teach and to learn; thus, teachers and students are similarly impacted by the threat of violence and harm.

The containment of violence has always been a primary concern for society. Throughout history, communities have best controlled violence by promoting the cooperation and collaboration of diverse interests and civic organizations. Within the past decade, there has been considerable national discussion regarding school violence. The education, law enforcement, and youth-serving agencies of Salem and Keizer, Oregon, have notably contributed to this discussion by initiating and developing one of the first collaborative systems to address the issue.

Initially funded and led by the Salem-Keizer School District in 2000, it was originally called the Salem-Keizer Student Threat Assessment System and is most commonly known throughout the nation as the Salem System. As the system was implemented throughout rural school districts in the mid-Willamette Valley (an effort conducted by the Willamette Education Service District), the official title changed to the Mid-Valley Student Threat Assessment System.

Recently the system has also become known as the Cascade Model for Student Threat Assessment because of its increased use by many of the school districts throughout the Pacific Northwest. Within this manual, we will simply refer to it as the STAS (Student Threat Assessment System).

STAS is a set of assessment and safety-planning procedures overseen and administered by a unique collaborative community team composed of schools, law enforcement, public mental health, and juvenile justice services. The primary goal of the system is to prevent and defuse threats to the physical and emotional safety of students and adults in our schools and community. Furthermore, the system reduces the overreaching responses of school zero-tolerance policies that often result in an inflated number of students identified as potentially dangerous and thus lead to an overreliance upon expulsion to resolve school safety concerns.

Threats are defined as situations that are at risk for outcome of aggression. The team examines those situations for factors that increase the likelihood of aggression. Once identified, those risk factors are reduced through the development of a management plan that directly addresses each factor through increased protective factors, increased supervision, and the introduction of intervention to decrease aggravating elements within the school, home, and community. This directly decreases fear-related distractions within the academic setting and thus improves the education environment for everyone.

The STAS process gathers the different perspectives of a school site–based multidisciplinary team to complete a Level 1 Threat Assessment with intervention strategies that are appropriate to the risk level. If further assessment is needed, the case is referred to the community-based multiagency team to complete a Level 2 assessment and consult on community resources. Thus, the two-level process efficiently maximizes school and community resources by determining the level of supervision and the intensity of intervention required to decrease the risk and ensure needed support.

The team-based investigation process is based upon assessment that determines the level of risk posed by a situation involving one or more students as opposed to other threat assessment instruments that profile students who appear to have characteristics that may predict future violence. The team-based decision making and supervision planning is based upon the assessment's indications of risk, the escalation of that risk, and the protective supports and strategies needed to decrease that risk.

Simply put, the objectives are:

1. Identify and assess threats of potentially harmful or lethal behavior and determine the level of concern and action required.
2. Organize resources and strategies to manage situations involving students that pose threats to other students, staff, and the community.
3. Maintain a sense of psychological safety among our students, teachers, and parents, thus fostering a learning environment that allows for teaching and learning that is free of the distraction caused by fear.

The system operates within a community that has centralized education resources, risk management resources, public mental health services, and the leadership of law enforcement. However, the model has also been used to address the needs of rural communities with limited resources or resources contracted through providers located in larger urban centers.

Regardless of the community setting, some sort of community-based Level 2 assessment team is essential to the system as a source of support to the schools and as a means of organizing resource options. An example of a Level 2 team is the Mid-Valley Student Threat Assessment Team or MVSTAT noted earlier in this chapter. Assembled in 2000, this threat assessment team, which used the STAS, was the first of its kind and has since been used as a template by dozens of school districts throughout the region as well as nationally. The team's membership is:

- Salem-Keizer School District
- Willamette Educational Services District (WESD)
- Marion County Sheriff's Office
- Salem Police Department
- Keizer Police Department
- Oregon Judicial Department
- Marion County Children's Mental Health
- Polk County Children's Mental Health
- Marion County Juvenile Department
- Polk County Juvenile Department
- Oregon Youth Authority
- Chemeketa Community College

The system offers several benefits:

1. It shares ownership, responsibility, and liability. With a multiagency membership and the support from the guidelines of the Safe School Initiative (Fein et al., 2002) and the FBI (O'Toole, 2000), agencies are offered the confidence of knowing that they are in good company and that no one person or agency shoulders the weight of decisions.
2. It is multidiscipline and multiagency. Such a process allows many different professional perspectives and disciplines.
3. It is expeditious but methodical. The response time can be within the day, allowing efficient safety planning, supervision, and necessary intervention. Considering the information time frame of past school shootings, an assessment model that supports an efficient and expeditious process will be far more effective than one that requires a complex or time-consuming process.
4. It is maintained by community collaboration and ownership. This decreases the pressure and worry within the schools and also lowers the potential conflict between schools and parents. It takes the focus or blame from being solely on the schools and brings community into the equation, allowing for a more united stand.

5. It identifies risk in clear terms. Clarity of language is more easily communicated to parents, teachers, and students.
6. Interventions and supervision strategies are fitting to the situation and accurately address risk. Thus, knee-jerk overreactions are avoided, and those involved can have an accurate and realistic understanding of the problem and needed solutions.
7. It safely keeps many students in school who would otherwise be removed through expulsion or by other means. Approximately nine out of ten MV-STAT assessments conclude with a supervision plan that is implemented at an education site.
8. It increases both the physical safety and the psychological safety of a school. A sense of safety is essential to a successful learning and teaching climate for students and staff.
9. It is derived from several significant research sets. (See References and Additional Readings.)
10. This type of system is recommended by the U.S. Departments of Education and Justice, NAAG, IACLEA, NASPA, MHEC, and others.

In response to a survey administered in 2005 by the University of Oregon Institute on Violence and Destructive Behavior, more than 94 percent of school administrators and counselors responding from the mid-Willamette Valley stated that:

1. STAS effectively identified potentially dangerous students and situations.
2. STAS had positive effects on school safety.
3. STAS provided important information necessary for support, discipline, and placement decisions.
4. STAS fulfills a valuable role in schools.

In the same survey, 90 percent of administrators reported that STAS increased efficient coordination with law enforcement and mental health. The survey indicated that school administrators and counselors strongly endorse the system and believe it plays an important role in maintaining safety in their schools and supporting referred students. Nearly all the respondents stated that the procedures were respectful of the student and his or her family. Finally, 95 percent stated that the system provided timely information essential for support and service decisions.

The anecdotal information from respondents reported high satisfaction with "the collaboration between school and agency specialists" as well as the improved access to community resources, networking, and a variety of ideas and perspectives for available potential help and services.

Based upon the start-up experiences of the MVSTAT, any school district or organization considering this system should expect the following challenges (further addressed in chapter 7):

1. Justification of need
2. Securing authorization from authority and the community
3. Securing community ownership, commitment, and responsibility
4. Organization of available resources
5. Designing of the system and articulation of the process
6. Training and the distribution of information
7. Continued maintenance and troubleshooting

One challenge not addressed above, but one that may be the system's greatest hurdle, is the "code of silence." This code is often followed by students and adults who believe that it is a sign of weakness or disloyalty to report or "tell" on others who are considering potentially harmful actions.

This code, however, has always been a feature of our interpersonal relationships because friends and family naturally protect each other, and the social system that supports them, from outside influences and forces. As humans evolved socially, their community's safety was better served by trusting its "business" to internal rather than external control. People were safer with those they knew than with those they knew little about. Thus, people, and especially young people, are naturally inclined to distrust those who are outside their circle of camaraderie, even if those people hold trustworthy positions of authority (such as school officials or the police).

This explains why school safety programs that encourage students to inform authority of dangerous student situations are in conflict with the code of silence and often fall short of their intended outcomes. It has only been within the last decade that some of our students have embraced the idea that school safety transcends the code and thus the stigma of being the one who informs.

While students continue to maintain their silence concerning each other's drug and alcohol use (they do not see the immediacy of the risk), many students have begun to realize the importance of sharing information about more immediately harmful behavior, such as suicide, physical assault, or even homicidal ideas. They understand that remaining silent interferes with the security and safety of everyone within the student population. Furthermore, they know that students considering such acts will greatly benefit from an intervention that stops them short of acting in a manner that will drastically change their lives and the lives of others.

This new awareness is due, in part, to the efforts of school staff and parents who are challenging the code. Unfortunately, it is also due to the tragedies witnessed when information is not shared or is ignored.

As a feature of the system's third objective, "psychological safety," any threat assessment team should encourage their community to applaud students and parents who understand that school safety is the responsibility of all. Educators and law enforcement must continue to encourage all students, parents, and the community to report any information about a situation that may be potentially violent or seriously harmful to any person. While there are many kinds of potentially violent or harmful situations, the following are three examples that should always be reported:

1. Thoughts or plans for committing a violent attack (addressed within this manual)
2. Suicidal ideas, intentions, or plans
3. Sexual aggression

School and community efforts should continually encourage anyone with concerns about youth (or adults) who may be considering any of the above-noted actions, or any action that could result in serious harm to themselves or others, to report the information to the police or a school staff member (preferably a school administrator). If concern is imminent, the report should be made immediately and directly through phoning 911.

To summarize, the Mid-Valley Student Threat Assessment System provides support to schools in assessing and managing potentially violent situations. The STAS process provides a framework for effective communication within a collaboration of youth-serving agencies such as education, law enforcement, the juvenile department, mental health, and child welfare.

The system also provides clear procedures for the timely, effective, and defensible assessment and management of threats in a manner that helps keep schools safe and continues the education opportunities of all students. In this manner, the process helps schools and multiagency teams develop interventions that assist the student(s) in remaining engaged in positive school experiences.

Finally, it is important to remember that the system is not a complete violence prevention strategy. Instead, STAS is most effective when schools use it in conjunction with universal violence prevention strategies that create a safe and caring school culture. The following is adapted from Safe Schools Initiative (Fein et al., 2002) and suggests that a successful school climate is accomplished by:

1. Assessing the emotional climate and then ensuring that staff, parents, and students understand the importance of listening and paying attention to the communications of students…especially communications that indicate

distress, fear, revenge, and hostility. An assessment of the emotional climate can be done through anonymous survey, anecdotal observation, or the compilation of student complaints and activity reports.

2. Adopting a strong but caring position against the "code of silence," especially as it pertains to lethal behavior like suicide and violence.
3. Prevention and intervention programs that address bullying.
4. Involving all members of the school community in creating a safe and respectful school climate.
5. Develop trusting relationships between each student and at least one adult at school.
6. Creating mechanisms for sustaining a safe school climate, such as a threat assessment system.

In other words, the safest schools have plans in place to prevent violence, identify persons at risk, intervene with risk concerns as they are indicated or develop, respond to violent acts if they occur, and recover from an event should it take place. The primary focus of this manual is to provide a template for a "mechanism" that sustains a safe school climate (#6 above). It will also address a few other items on the above list; however, it is not intended to be a complete reference for school climate improvement.

With improvements in school safety and learning climates free of serious threat or the distraction of fear, the learning experience will be far more successful and enjoyable to all students, and the work experience will be more satisfying for teachers and other staff. Furthermore, anger and aggression can be appropriately managed and thus, the grievous consequences avoided.

Chapter Two

A Brief History of the System

John Van Dreal

The system was designed in 1999 and 2000. At that time many educators were concerned with the "epidemic" of school shootings, and although injury resulting from violence was far more likely to occur outside of the school than within its environment, the adverse impact of rampage school shootings on the national psyche was undeniable. Furthermore, school violence has decreased within the past decade and yet shootings do continue to occur, elevating our concerns and holding us invested in a means by which we can decrease it or even eliminate it.

What was the "epidemic" of school shootings? The media coined the term to describe a series of school shootings that occurred in the mid-1990s at Moses Lake, Washington; Bethel, Alaska; Paducah, Kentucky; Jonesboro, Arkansas...and ended in 1999 with the events at Columbine High School in Littleton, Colorado. This "epidemic" included Oregon's own rampage shooting in Springfield. In truth, school violence was not new to America in the 1990s.

The first record of a violent attack on an American school and its youth is noted in August of 1764 by Benjamin Franklin in the *Pennsylvania Gazette*. The event, referred to as the Enoch Brown School massacre, took place just after the end of the French-Indian War, during Pontiac's Rebellion (a result of the hostilities that continued after the treaty was signed). On the morning of July 26, 1764, four men from the Delaware American Indian tribe entered a school house and attacked the teacher, Enoch Brown, and student body with tomahawks, scalping Mr. Brown and all twelve children. Mr. Brown and ten of the children died, while two children survived.

In 1927, forty-five people, mostly students, were killed and fifty-eight others injured when the disgruntled custodian and school board member, angry about his increased taxes and the foreclosure of his farm, killed his wife and burned his farmhouse then dynamited the school, shot the principal, and then shot himself.

In 1966, fourteen people were killed and thirty-two wounded in an attack at the University of Texas. On January 29, 1979, an adolescent female, expelled from the district's high school, attacked Cleveland Elementary School in San Diego, California, killing the principal and custodian and wounding nine others.

School violence is not new to our communities, but it is uncommon. In fact, school deaths or serious injury resulting from violence is statistically quite rare. During the worst two years of the epidemic, 1998 and 1999, one homicide occurred within the schools for every two million students who remained safe. In other words, there was a one in two million chance of being murdered within a school. At that time, a student's chances of being murdered were approximately forty times higher outside of the schools. Schools were then and are today very safe places for our youth.

Still, when a school shooting takes place, it has a profound impact on our communities and country. Teaching and learning slows or even stops as Americans view the news with cognitive shock over the possibility of such acts. It seems personal to all Americans, as they see images of victims who look like students or teachers they know and work with daily. Even the perpetrators look familiar...alike in appearance and dress to many students that educators work with on a daily basis.

Today, while even less frequent, school violence and rampage shootings still occur in our public schools and more recently on our college campuses. A greater number of shootings would likely occur if it were not for the often-untold successes of interrupted or deterred attacks. Violence has been averted because of an increasingly vigilant student body, the presence of law enforcement in the schools, and surveillance systems such as the one outlined in this manual.

At the time of the initial work on this system, many educational policy responses to the shootings ranged from reactionary measures to positions of complete denial. Most initial programs were well intended but ineffective, and the initial "risk" checklists are thankfully gone now, as many districts pursue a more defensible and competent process (Van Dreal et al., 2005).

Furthermore, students continued to use threatening language as a means of communicating everything from terms of endearment to actual predictions of aggression. Threats were commonplace in the schools and community then, and they continue to be today. Then, as now, many educators were frequently faced with the question of how to respond and when to treat threats as serious.

In 1999, the Oregon legislature responded to public pressure regarding school violence and passed legislation mandating schools to form alliances with law enforcement, mental health, district attorney's offices, and juvenile justice departments to build policies and procedures that would promote safe and caring school campuses. Called HB 3444 and 3047, the bills stressed staff reporting methods, student removal, mental health evaluations, and potential victim's parent notification.

Unfortunately the legislation, while well intended, did not provide adequate outlines for programs or systems and appeared to rely on "mental health evaluation" for the answers needed to determine safe school procedures. Within a few years, many school districts were finding that reliance on such evaluations was expensive, time consuming, and often required lengthy waits for appointments and subsequent safety planning meetings.

Many students were held out of school for days, sometimes weeks, before their risk was evaluated and return planning could take place (Van Dreal et al., 2005). Additionally, many mental health practitioners were uncomfortable administering risk assessments based upon psychological indicators alone.

These concerns and legislation, along with the desire to create a psychologically safe environment where teachers and students alike could be free to teach and learn without concern for their personal safety causing distraction and fear, motivated the creation of an efficient, time-sensitive threat assessment system for youth.

The project was led by Salem-Keizer with the collaboration of a team of youth-serving agencies consisting of Marion County Sheriff's Department, Salem Police Department, Keizer Police Department, Marion County Children's Mental Health Department, Polk County Children's Mental Health Department, Marion County Juvenile Department, Polk County Juvenile Department, and Marion County Department of Human Services.

This collaboration was fortunate in that the Marion County Threat Advisory Team (MTAT) already existed to address adult threats in the community. MTAT was formed in 1998 through the partnership of law enforcement, the state courts, and Salem-Keizer School District. It was the first team of its kind and was organized to address threats to the courts and to public officials, threats in the workplace, and threats of domestic violence and stalking.

Using MTAT as an example, the Student Threat Assessment System proceeded. The project was led with the question "is school violence solely a school district problem or is it a community problem?" All agencies participating agreed that, while students are housed in schools during the day, the entire community is responsible for the problem. As a commitment to this ownership, the collaboration began a series of focus groups and discussions to develop the system.

The development process involved a thorough survey of available research and best practice recommendations (see References) as well as the consultation of local practitioners who regularly assess or encounter potentially violent situations involving youth. Finally the system was refined and completed through committee work with school and public administrators, school counselors, social workers, school psychologists, risk management personnel, mental health practitioners, juvenile justice probation officers, and law enforcement officers.

The system began operation within the Salem-Keizer School District in the fall of 2000. A year later, the Willamette Education Service District joined the team and began implementing the system throughout the rural school districts in Marion and Polk counties.

The system in place today includes the Adult Threat Advisory Team and the Student Threat Assessment Team. Both teams operate through assessment protocols, supervision and management consultation, and access to available community resources. The system is now operated through a collaboration of the public agencies that serve youth and adults in our community. Members of this collaboration are trained to the highest standards available and are available to schools for assessment, consultation, and resource development.

Most recently, the system has been adapted for several of Willamette Valley's higher education campuses and their security needs.

Like most community collaborations, both threat assessment teams encountered barriers and hurdles. Foremost among the challenges were lack of available services, differences in agency philosophies, an absence of policies to address issues regarding record sharing and confidentiality, information storage, lack of resources to support information needs, and funding limitations.

The process for overcoming these barriers required commitment on the part of each agency as well as top management support of the team and its endeavor. The resulting infrastructure continues to need occasional reconsideration; however, its strength today is an example of systems change and a disciplined approach to public and school safety.

Section II

Foundations

Chapter Three

Supportive Research and Recommendations

John Van Dreal

This chapter highlights several studies and research sets that have greatly influenced campus threat assessment today. The chapter is by no means an exhaustive review or even a detailed review, but is a means by which the information can be outlined and presented as a foundational source for the following chapters of protocol and system.

THE EXCEPTIONAL CASE STUDY PROJECT

The Exceptional Case Study Project (ECSP) was initially completed by the United States Secret Service in 1998. The project analyzed eighty-three persons who had engaged in assassination attacks or near-attack behaviors from the previous forty-six years. The results of the study provided an objectified definition of targeted violence and concluded that targeted attackers do not have consistent profiles.

The study also noted that mental illness plays almost no role in determining violence potential but did identify and emphasize the concept of "attack-related behaviors." Finally, the study noted that most attackers consider many targets prior to attacks and that risk is best determined through an investigation of the attack-related behaviors as they relate to the potential attacker's ideation (Fein et al., 1995). The work done by the ECSP produced several reports and products (Fein et al., 1995, and Borum et al., 1999) that are excellent references for further study. More information can be found at www .secretservice.gov/ntac.

DEPARTMENT OF JUSTICE/
FEDERAL BUREAU OF INVESTIGATION

In 2000, the National Center for the Analysis of Violent Crime (NCAVC) published a monograph authored by supervisory special agent Mary Ellen O'Toole called *The School Shooter: A Threat Assessment Perspective*. The text addressed targeted school shootings through a "Four-Pronged Assessment Approach." The following is an adaptation of the identified factors, and while the list clearly notes traits and features common to most at-risk youth issues, these factors are warning signs that increase in weight and importance when combined with threatening situations (the monograph can be viewed in full at www.fbi.gov/publications/school/school2.pdf or by following the reference citation).

Personality Traits and Behavior

- Leakage: Intentionally or unintentionally revealing thoughts, attitudes, and intentions. Leakage may be expressed as subtle threats, boasts, innuendos, predictions, ultimatums, and may even be in the form of a variety of possible communications such as writings, songs, texts, emails, art, or other visual media.
- Low Tolerance for Frustration: Easily insulted, easily agitated.
- Poor Coping Skills: Exaggerated, immature, disproportionate, or inappropriate responses.
- Lack of Resiliency: Unable to bounce back from disappointment or failure.
- Failed Love Relationship or Injustice Collector: Cannot forgive or forget. Holds on to a grudge or grievance with animosity.
- Signs of Depression: May not be diagnosed. Can be atypical or difficult to detect.
- Narcissism: Self-centered, lacks insight into self and others, superficial, blames others, is self-important.
- Alienation: Estranged and separate…marginalized, not just a loner.
- Dehumanizes Others: Lack of empathy or recognition for others as humans.
- Exaggerated Sense of Entitlement: Expectations of special treatment… above the rules.
- Attitude of Superiority: A view of self as smarter, better, and superior than others.
- Exaggerated or Pathological Need for Attention: Attention can be positive or negative.
- Externalizes Blame: Does not take responsibility for actions or admit wrongdoing. Continually places blame on others.
- Masks Low Self-Esteem: Actions, statements, and bravado veil an underlying low or wounded self-esteem.

- Anger Management Problems: Temper outbursts, underlying anger issues, or anger that is incongruent with the cause.
- Intolerance: Expressions or actions of intolerance or disdain for individuals or groups.
- Inappropriate Humor: Jokes tend to be macabre, insulting, belittling, or mean.
- Seeks to Manipulate Others: Ongoing behavior that cons or manipulates others, often to their discomfort.
- Lack of Trust: Chronically suspicious of others' motives and intentions.
- Closed Social Group: Socially introverted with acquaintances rather than friends. Or may associate with a small, marginalized group.
- Change of Behavior: Dramatic and recent.
- Rigid and Opinionated: Judgmental and cynical.
- Unusual Interest in Sensational Violence: School shootings or other publicized violence. May even express admiration for violent figures.
- Fascination with Violence-Filled Entertainment: Interest exceeds the normal interest of age and peer group. Interest may even be rehearsal.
- Negative Role Models: Hitler, Satan, fantasy characters, other school shooters, and so on.
- Behavior Appears Relevant to Carrying Out a Threat: Activities suggest rehearsal, practice, planning, and preparation.

Family Dynamics

- Turbulent Parent-Child Relationship: Considerable distress and difficulty within the parent-child relationship, including the possibility of violence in the home.
- Acceptance of Pathological Behavior: Parents are not concerned with the student's socially maladjusted or antisocial behavior or ideas.
- Access to Weapons: Locked or "secure" weapons within a home are still accessible to a resourceful youth.
- Lack of Intimacy: A lack of closeness and connection within the family.
- Student "Rules the Roost": Parents do not discipline or are afraid to discipline, impose boundaries, or require commitment and responsibility.
- No Limits or Monitoring of TV and Internet: Poor parental supervision and control.

School Dynamics

- Student's Attachment to School: Detached from school, peers, and staff.
- Tolerance for Disrespectful Behavior: There is little to prevent or punish disrespectful behavior between students and groups of students.

- Inequitable Discipline: Either real or perceived inequities, based upon social status, athletic value, race, and so on, within the application of discipline.
- Inflexible Culture: Official or unofficial patterns of behavior that secure values and relationships that are static, unyielding, and insensitive to changes in society, needs, and demographics.
- Pecking Order among Students: Certain groups are officially or unofficially given more prestige and respect than others.
- Code of Silence: Students adhere to a rule that it is not "cool" or okay to inform on peers, regardless of the risk being posed.
- Unsupervised Computer Access: Poor supervision or control of computer or Internet use.

Social Dynamics

- Media, Entertainment, Technology: Easy and unmonitored access to movies, TV, computer games, and Internet with themes or images of extreme violence.
- Peer Groups: Intense and exclusive involvement with peers who share a fascination with extreme violence and extremist beliefs.
- Drugs and Alcohol: Use, but more important, changes in a student's drug and alcohol use.
- Outside Interests: Interests that are socially agitating, antisocial, or destructive.
- The Copycat Effect: Admiring and wanting to repeat or outdo previous acts of notorious violence.

SAFE SCHOOL INITIATIVE

In 2002, the United States Secret Service, in a joint effort with the United States Department of Education, completed the final report and recommendations from the Safe School Initiative (Vossekuil et al., 2002; Fein et al., 2002). The study analyzed thirty-seven school shooting incidents involving forty-one students between 1974 and 2002. The following is an abbreviation of those findings. Further information can be found at www.secretservice .gov/ntac.shtml or by following the reference citation.

- The shootings were rarely impulsive. The shooters did not simply "snap" or impulsively decide to set out on a spree of rage and murder. The shootings were the result of a process of thinking and behaving, beginning with an idea and progressing through the development of a plan, and on to action. Almost all events were preceded by attack-related behaviors such as target research, the acquisition of weapons, rehearsal, simulation, and scheduling.

- There are no consistent profiles of school shooters. In fact, to date, there continues to be a growing variation in their demographics. Furthermore, even if we add the school shootings that have occurred since this study, the sample set is still far too small to draw or predict a set of instrumental features or profile traits. Thus, rather than examining the characteristics or "type" of student who would attack a school, this study suggests investigating the circumstances that indicate a progression toward an attack or accelerate its likelihood.
- School shooters had difficulty coping with loss and failure. They perceived or experienced major loss and had poor adaptive skills and poor coping strategies. Approximately 75 percent of shooters had a history of suicidal thoughts, gestures, or attempts. Most of them displayed signs of depression or were diagnosed with depression.
- Shooters experienced or perceived severe longstanding rejection, persecution, or bullying by peers. (Katherine Newman [2004], whose material was not a part of the Safe School Initiative, suggests that direct bullying was not a key factor in every case because many shooters may have experienced social rejection and perceived it as bullying or torment. Furthermore, she notes that many of the school shooters were noted by staff and students to be bullies themselves.)
- The motives and justifications were mostly based on revenge and problem solving with a solution plan that ended in violence.
- Peers frequently knew of the shooting plan ahead of time, and some even collaborated or assisted on details or scheduling. The adolescent code of silence was, unfortunately, very much in existence.
- All attackers used guns. Most shooters had ready access to guns in their own home or the home of a relative or friend. Those that did not have an available gun made considerable efforts to acquire one or more. Two-thirds of the school shooters used handguns, one-third used rifles, and half used both handguns and rifles.
- Most attackers did not directly threaten their targets prior to the attack.
- All shooters were previously identified as a concern for parents and/or teachers or peers, though not necessarily for potential violence.
- Despite prompt law enforcement responses, most attacks were short in duration and were stopped by some means other than law enforcement.

RAMPAGE SHOOTINGS

In her book *Rampage: The Social Roots of School Shootings* (2004), Katherine Newman suggests that school shooters, through a violent rampage executed at the most public of institutions and at the center of their social universe (the school), are altering their social reputation. Within small communities, there is no social stage comparable to the school, assuring that a rural school shooting will draw considerable attention. Through that act of highly public violence, they hope to reinvent themselves as antiheroes and thus reverse years of labeling as social failures. She identifies five necessary, but not sufficient, conditions for what she terms as a rampage school shooting.

1. The attacker is marginalized within the social world that has importance or value. Acts of bullying and social exclusion lead to further marginalization and increase frustration, self-pity, and depression.
2. School shooters have psychological problems and/or vulnerability. This is similar to what Andre Simons refers to as "brittleness." Mental illness, severe depression, and abuse all decrease emotional coping reserves and thus magnify the impact of marginalization. While many students are marginalized, those who have low psychological coping reserves are the least likely to survive it without long-term scars and resentments.
3. Cultural or media models that solve problems through the application of violence are readily available as examples for getting even, releasing discomfort, or elevating social status. The glamorizing and sensationalizing of school shootings through film, news media, and the web offer "scripts" that propose the use of violence as a means of proving masculine fortitude, lack of conformity, or even elevating social status.
4. The surveillance of student behavior, communication, and activity is an extremely important feature of any school safety system. Shootings occur when systems intended to identify troubled youth are ineffective or nonexistent. Postincident information suggests that many shooters would likely have stopped somewhere along the continuum of targeted behavior if others had not continued to provoke them and dare them to act out while surveillance systems either failed to detect the growing risk or were not in place.
5. The availability of weapons (almost always guns) is necessary to the execution of a violent plan. Students who are seriously considering a rampage shooting will go to extreme efforts to obtain the necessary weapons, so the standard efforts of control, such as the use of gun safes or the elimination of guns from a home, are not a sufficient intervention within the context of firm resolve and commitment.

In her summary, Newman notes that the research clearly suggests that attempting to predict future violence through the limitations of psychological examination alone is unreliable. The best approach is to intercept the communication flow and examine the circumstances of threatening situations.

OTHER INFORMATION

Recently, supervisory special agent Andre Simons of the FBI Behavioral Analysis Unit has noted the following factors that appear to elevate risk. Some of the information is anecdotal and taken from his observations and experiences, and other observations are derived from SSA Simons's work on the recently published report *Campus Attacks: Targeted Violence Affecting Institutions of Higher Education*, issued jointly by the U.S. Secret Service, the U.S. Department of Education, and the FBI (April 2010):

- Consistent with previously published research, some individuals who demonstrate an intent and ability to attack may have experienced significant personal stress, humiliation, and/or perceived failure prior to the attack or attempted attack.
- Some school attacks involving suicides may have become suicide attempts externalized to homicidal acts, consistent with the externalization of blame (termed "aggressive martyrdom" by Reid Meloy).
- Some attacks may represent psychologically transformational acts, whereby the subject views the violent attack as a bridge between an intolerable situation and desired power, relief, and infamy.
- Many school shooters appear to have been brittle, accumulating injustices and lacking coping skills or prosocial problem-solving strategies needed to appropriately address the accumulated injustices they have experienced or imagined.
- In some cases, warning signs may have been indicated through the presence of leakage, which included hyper profanity, negative emotional language, lack of future planning, weapons investigation or possession, and an inability to take personal responsibility for actions and outcomes. Recklessness, as demonstrated by high-risk behavior through financial, sexual, or recreational activities, may also have been a warning sign.
- In completed or attempted attacks, violence may have represented a solution to perceived problems and not necessarily a means by which to extort or negotiate a demand.
- There has been an increase in the popularity of video wills or manifestos. These legacy tokens suggest the attackers' desire for infamy and notoriety, particularly in cases where the videos or letters are delivered to media agencies prior to the attack.
- Some shooters have affected what Reid Meloy refers to as a "pseudo-commando" appearance with a warrior mentality evidenced in recordings, writings, or attitude prior to or during the attack.

• While all threats should be taken seriously and examined immediately, in some cases, an anonymous, direct threat that provides specific information regarding the date and time of attack may be counterproductive to a true intent of attack, as it inevitably results in increased security countermeasures. However, a leakage of intent provided through conversation, warnings from one to another ("you may not want to be at school on Tuesday"), or other modes may be very concerning and should be addressed through immediate threat management considerations. As noted previously, threats are always reviewed within a contextually driven process.

Sharon Smith, in her article "From Violent Words to Violent Deeds" (2008), noted the importance of examining the relationship between cognitive complexity and hostility. Plans involving cognitive complexity and hostility that is ambivalent (not focused, not fixed, and not specific) tend not to lead to violent outcomes, while cognitive complexity combined with low ambivalent hostility actually translates to a higher likelihood of predatory violence.

To summarize, the following list of factors is an attempt to assemble the available information regarding targeted school violence into a set of basic questions. Any protocol or system of school threat assessment should begin, at a minimum, with a foundation drawn from this list.

1. Have there been threatening communications suggesting a potential violent attack? What kind of communication has the student made regarding their intention to harm others? Is the communication a statement of anger such as "I'm going to kill you..." or is it an expression that involves details of planning or ongoing consideration of an attack? Communications may include verbal expressions, artwork, email, Internet messaging, texting, written language exercises, or any other medium of communication.

   A communication can also be made by indirect, veiled, or casual references to possible harmful events, ominous warnings, or references to previously occurring violent events such as school or community shootings. A threat does not have to be specifically stated to be of concern, nor does it have to be stated or implied within the campus setting. Monitoring communication is a key factor in assessing threat. Interrupting communication flow and understanding the context of the communication is a first step in assessing risk.

2. Are there indications of a specific target or targets? Is there an ongoing consideration or focus on a particular person, group, or student body? If the situation is absent a notable target, it is likely a situation that revolves around reactive aggression, used as a means to bully, intimidate, confront, or defend interests and wants. Planned attacks cannot take place without targets.

3. Are there indications of a motive, goal, or justification for a serious or lethal attack? If there is a focus on a specific target or targets, then there is very likely a motive. While there can certainly be many motives for acting out violently or aggressively, the most common is the need to establish or reestablish control as indicated by revenge, a vendetta for lost love, humiliation, or the desire to prove bravery after making a threat or taking a dare.

   Examining motive and justification from the perspective of the youth is another step toward understanding the threat and the level of risk. If the situation is absent a motive, then it may be a situation involving reactive aggression or the affectation of rage. Reactive aggressive and violent bravado often have triggers that agitate the situation rapidly. Such triggers are usually not motives but should still be identified in order to avoid or eliminate them in the future.

4. Are there any indications of attack-related behavior that increase the possibility of violence occurring…such as a plan, acquiring or attempting to acquire weapons, rehearsing the attack, simulation of the attack, or other preparations such as scheduling the event?

   A communication that threatens an attack is only an expression and does not suggest a "posed threat" unless there are behaviors supporting the intent to carry out the attack. Many threats are not stated with clearly expressed language but are indicated by veiled threats and attack-related behavior. Attack-related behavior may be, but is not limited to, the following:

   - *A plan (complex or simple) to carry out a targeted act of aggression against a specific individual, group, or student body.* A plan would have a sequence of actions necessary for its success and is almost always fueled by a motive. The more plausible the plan, the greater the risk.
   - *The acquisition of a weapon, the attempted acquisition of a weapon, or research about how to acquire a weapon.* If the threat is the use of physical force to the point of serious or lethal injury, then the physical force is the weapon.
   - *The rehearsal of the event or a similar event.* Rehearsal is like simulation or practice. Rehearsal or simulation is often necessary before a targeted event can be completely planned and carried out. Rehearsal can be indicated through art, fantasy games, writing, or film projects. It can also be indicated by the use of movies or Internet sites that have themes and sequences of violence that allow the simulation of targeted and violent acts or through first-person shooter video games that also allow for simulation of sequential and violent acts. However, it must be noted that the use of such games or films as entertainment does not lead or cause

students to act out violently. Their use is only attack-related behavior when it serves as rehearsal or simulation and practice.

- *Scheduling an attack.* Scheduling the act is sometime indicated through vague communication or actually noted in clear detail. Sometimes the schedule is flexible, awaiting a triggering event (teasing, rejection, loss) that further justifies the violence and locks it in as the only solution.

5. Are actions and behaviors consistent with communications? If threats are made but there are not attack-related behaviors, motives, or a specific target(s) consistent with that threat, then risk decreases. Many threats that lack attack-related behavior are likely to be a means of communicating dissatisfaction, attention seeking, expressing anger, releasing stress, or even an affectation of strength or power (bravado).
6. Is there peer collaboration? Are peers aware of or concerned about a potential attack? Other students can be extremely important in information gathering.
7. Does the situation involve a student or students who are out of alternatives and low on reserves? For example, if the student is still willing to speak with the school counselor, he or she is not out of alternatives. Does the situation involve a marginalized student who is completely disenfranchised and without a relationship connection to prosocial adults? Is the student low on psychological reserves and out of acceptable coping strategies? Are there indications of hopeless, stressfully overwhelming, or desperate situations (either real or perceived)?

   Mental illness, severe depression, and abuse decrease emotional, psychological, and coping reserves. Low reserves tend to magnify rejection and marginalization. As students lose hope of resolving stressful or overwhelming situations through acceptable social or coping skills, they are more likely to engage in desperate solutions and last-ditch efforts to take control. It is important to note that the point of this question is to examine the perception of the person or party you are concerned with, not necessarily what is realistically observed or known by others (staff, parents, other students, or the community). Is the student willing to accept the consequences of carrying out the threat?
8. Are there indications of suicidal ideation? Is there a history of suicidal ideation, gestures, references, or intent? A desire to die, be killed by another, or commit suicide combined with a threat to harm others increases the overall risk, especially if the suicidal behavior is one feature of a plan to kill others and carry out revenge or justice. If there is a risk of suicide, always proceed with legal and agency policy for further assessment.

9. Are there personality or behavioral traits, family dynamics, school system issues, or social dynamics that lead to a more vulnerable and potentially dangerous situation? O'Toole's work (noted above) identifies many traits and dynamics that increase risk and vulnerability.

The lessons identified in this chapter's review of research, along with the basic concepts identified in the following chapter, are the foundation for the assessment process, the investigative focus, and the formation of the protocols found throughout the remainder of the manual. For further study, see References or go to http://studentthreatassessment.org for links.

Chapter Four

Basic Concepts

John Van Dreal

This chapter examines the concepts that are basic and foundational to threat assessment. An understanding of the basics is the best launching point from which to build a system. This chapter along with the previous chapter should provide most of what is needed to begin the work; however, further study through the sources listed within the reference section is recommended.

The defining information within this chapter is drawn from a number of experts, noted below and in the Acknowledgments section at the beginning of this manual. Information and links are also available at the website studentthreatassessment.org.

Before reviewing the information in this chapter, reflect on the risk factors identified in the previous chapter and consider the following six scenarios, making note of your concerns regarding risk. Keep your concerns in mind as you review the remainder of the manual, reconsidering your assessment of risk as you learn more about the application of the material into protocol and system.

1. Three high-school boys are engaging in violent and antisocial (rated M) first-person video games. They have also engaged in BB-gun wars after school. They collect and trade knives and are aggressive with each other, often frightening teachers with their bravado, vulgar language, and oppositional attitudes. Two of the boys play seasonal sports and the third is very involved with art and science. A few teachers have requested that the district expel or transfer all three students because they fear that "they are the kind of kids who shoot up schools."

2. One middle-school boy is found to have a large skinning knife in his backpack. He claims he used it the previous weekend while hunting with his

family, and the explanation is confirmed by his father. He has a school behavioral history of reckless and sometimes oppositional behavior, and he is
on medication for ADHD. His teachers are tired of managing his behavior.
His parents are cooperative most of the time but have grown irritated with
the referrals and behavioral consultations.

3. One high-school freshman boy brings a knife (with an eight-inch blade) to
school as a defensive means of protecting himself against an older male
bully who is tormenting him and extorting his lunch money. He has few
emotional or coping resources but does have one very positive relationship
with his English teacher. He has told other students that he is intending to
display the weapon as a means of warning and intimidating the bully away
from the ongoing harassment.

4. One middle-school girl with a history of social conflict and physical aggression is a known bully. Students have reported that she has been bringing a knife to school to intimidate other students. There is a rumor that she
has specifically threatened to stab a specific student, and that student will
no longer ride the bus.

5. One high-school boy has told two of his classmates that he would like to
shoot several other students as revenge for their socially rejecting behavior
and because several of them have called him "gay" when he is at his locker.
He has previously told his counselor that he has been frequently humiliated
and embarrassed but has stopped confiding in her and now states that the
social rejection is "no big deal." He has also noted on web blogs that he
will someday prove that he is not weak or afraid. He is somewhat marginalized due to his choice of other marginalized friends, and his social skills
are limited and rigid.

6. Two fifth-grade boys, both identified as emotionally disturbed and attending school in a self-contained classroom, are engaging each other in
daily conflict. One is very aggressive and uses combative talk to threaten
teachers and students if he does not get his way. He is extremely irritable
and has a very short fuse. The other is less aggressive, but if pushed, can
become extremely explosive and reactively aggressive. A few parents
of the other students have complained about the constant disruption,
and one parent has said that he thinks the second boy could be a school
shooter because he has few friends, is quiet, and can become so explosive. The two boys are headed for a major confrontation with each other.

A few of these six scenarios are fairly common within schools; a few are
not. The remainder of this chapter provides general concepts that should assist you as you begin to examine risk through a threat-assessment lens.

THREATS AND COMMUNICATION

Inappropriate Communication: Any unwarranted contact or approach that is strange, threatening, or ominously predictive and intended to unsettle or unnerve. These communications or actions are not simple expressions of opinion or objections but tend to cause pause or a sense of discomfort with the recipient (de Becker, 1998; Calhoun, 1998). The following are a few examples: references to death, weapons, or violence; previous violent acts; extreme or obsessive attention, admiration, or attention; stalking behavior or research of personal information; a sense of destiny shared with the target (that is not returned). Inappropriate communications can also be direct threats, indirect threats, veiled threats, and conditional threats (O'Toole, 2000):

- Direct Threat: A threat characterized by specifics noting intent to do harm and identifying both the victim and the perpetrator. Direct threats are clear and explicit (Calhoun, 1998). "On Monday, I'm going to bring a gun and shoot everyone at school."
- Indirect Threat: A threat is present but is ambiguous or otherwise unclear. The threat may be tentative with masked or evasive references to victim, perpetrator, plan, and justification, but the violence is definitely implied (O'Toole, 2000). "I have what I need to kill everyone in this class."
- Veiled Threat: A threat that implies violence but does not clearly threaten it. The threat may be characterized by specifics but vague in one of two ways: either uncertainty about who will carry out the threat or uncertainty about who will be the victim (de Becker, 1998; Calhoun, 1998). "You may not want to come to school on Tuesday. Something terrible may happen."
- Conditional Threat or Instrumental Threat: A threat made to control or influence the target's behavior (Meloy, 2000). A threat of harm or misfortune that will occur if another action is not taken or activity completed. The harm is conditional: "If you do not do ____ I will do ____ to you" (de Becker, 1998; Calhoun, 1998). A conditional threat can be either direct or veiled. "If you don't cancel graduation, people will get hurt."
- Expressive Threat: A threat that is based on emotion and often made an expression of anger, rage, or hatred or as a defense against fear or shame (Meloy, 2000). They can be recognized by their affective nature (i.e., "blowing off steam"). "I could kill you!"

THE AGGRESSION CONTINUUM

Doing the work of threat assessment can be complicated and confusing at first because the public tends to place almost every aggressive youth behavior into the category of dangerous. Many educators and parents frequently label students who make threats or act out as "violent." What does this mean, and is it even accurate? What, exactly, is aggression and when does aggression become violent and dangerous?

Forensic psychologist Eric M. Johnson has addressed this question through a continuum of behavior, noting the difference between mildly aggressive behavior, moderately aggressive behavior, and extreme forms of behavior (otherwise referred to as violence). By doing so, he has suggested the importance of avoiding the use of the label "violent" and using descriptors such as mild, medium, or extreme aggression and then defining them.

A youth should only be described as violent when the behavior clearly fits within extreme forms of aggression that have potential or intended outcomes that cause severe or lethal injury. (Since "violence" is the most common term used nationally for the description of aggressive behavior that is dangerous, this book will continue to use it interchangeably with extreme aggression.)

Aggression can be defined as harmful behavior directed at another person. An aggressive threat, then, is an expressed intention to act out that harmful behavior. Within this continuum, aggressive behavior ranges from high-frequency, low-impact actions such as pushing, slapping, biting, scratching, and kicking to lower-frequency, higher-impact actions such as beating, strangulation, stabbing, and shooting.

Some of the behavior, such as sexual coercion or fighting, may be within the range of extreme aggression depending upon the intent or the outcome (again, serious or lethal injury). Also, while there is a suggested progression of behavior from mild to extreme, the listed examples serve only as illustration and are not necessarily locked into their position within the continuum. In other words, hitting can be a mild, moderate, or even extreme form of aggression, depending upon the intention or the outcome of harm.

The point of the continuum is to illustrate that aggression is most concerning when it is intended to cause or results in serious or lethal injury. And at that point it is defined as extreme aggression—harmful behavior that is directed at another person(s) and causes or is intended to cause serious or lethal injury (Johnson, 2000). A violent threat, then, is an expressed intention to act out harmful behavior with the goal of severe or lethal injury. Figure 4.1 is an adaptation of Johnson's continuum, altered for application into a public education threat assessment system.

A common complication to this differentiation of behavior occurs when a youth is acting in an aggressive but nonviolent manner (pushing, shoving, or light fistfighting with another youth) and at the same time screaming verbal threats of violence ("I'm going to get my father's gun and blow your head off...") as an expression of bravado and affect. The task here is to match be-

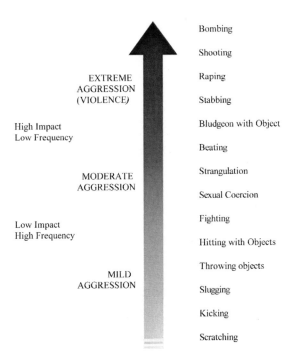

EXTREME
AGGRESSION
(VIOLENCE*)*

High Impact
Low Frequency

MODERATE
AGGRESSION

Low Impact
High Frequency

MILD
AGGRESSION

Bombing

Shooting

Raping

Stabbing

Bludgeon with Object

Beating

Strangulation

Sexual Coercion

Fighting

Hitting with Objects

Throwing objects

Slugging

Kicking

Scratching

Figure 4.1

havior with threat or intent, especially if the violent threat is a prediction of future violence ("I'm going to get a gun and blow your head off..."). Therein is the beginning of the assessment process.

Why is it important to accurately note the behavior and the level of intended or resulting physical harm? The label of "violent" is one that should only be used with consideration and caution, because if it is liberally spoken, it can create unnecessary panic, overreaction, and even lead to the misuse of valuable resources. While common moderately aggressive behavior such as fighting should always be of concern, it is in no way as concerning as extremely aggressive (or violent) behavior and thus should be addressed with consequences, discipline, and strategies that match its impact and risk.

Finally, it is always best to describe aggression in terms of mild, moderate, or extreme and note the likely seriousness of injury or potential injury.

CIRCUMSTANCES, CONTEXT, AND SITUATION

In addition to the differentiation between aggression and violence, our system is designed to assess circumstances involving individuals or groups rather

than assess individuals isolated from the circumstances that increase or de-
crease the risk they pose to others. This passage from *Threat Assessment in
Schools: A Guide to Managing Threatening Situations and to Creating Safe
School Climates* (Fein et al., 2002) summarizes this idea:

> The primary purpose of a threat assessment is to prevent targeted violence. The
> threat assessment process is centered upon analysis of the facts and evidence of
> behavior in a given situation. The appraisal of risk in a threat assessment focuses
> on actions, communications, and specific circumstances that suggest that an
> individual intends to mount an attack and is engaged in planning or preparing
> for that event.

In other words, it is the assessment of the "unique" interaction and dynamics between the perpetrator or attacker, the target, and the situation they share
(Mohandie, 2000). In threat assessment, the question being asked is "given
the circumstances, does the attacker 'pose' a threat or danger to others?" (de
Becker, 1998).

The question is answered by assessing the circumstances that include the
attacker, the target, and the dynamics of their relationship. The question is not
answered by evaluating whether or not the attacker is a "dangerous person" or
whether or not the attacker has expressed a direct threat. We cannot establish
a depth of concern by evaluating a student's appearance or words alone, but
we can establish a depth of concern based upon a student's behavior within
the circumstances of the threat.

To further illustrate the importance of viewing risk through context, consider the student who brings a knife to school. While the presence of a knife
at school is concerning, the risk associated with the knife depends upon
whether the knife was brought as a sort of show and tell, or if it was brought
as a means of self-defense or worse yet, as a means of directly threatening,
intimidating, or even assaulting another student.

A more dramatic example of the importance of context is the following
story regarding my son, my father, and a rather archaic method of teaching
a child to swim.

Several years ago, I was attempting to teach my son to swim (he was
nine years old and still very hesitant to risk a journey into the deep-end
of a swimming pool). My father, George, who was a lifeguard during his
military years and who apparently grew up as an excellent swimmer, was
visiting for the summer and noted my son's lack of ambition and courage
regarding the water.

On one afternoon we were lounging by the edge of the neighborhood
pool and I mentioned my frustration at my failed attempts, including ongoing swim lessons, to encourage my son to learn to swim. George said, "You

know, John, I learned to swim when my father put me in a boat, paddled me out into a lake, and threw me in the water." And I said, "Hey, George, maybe Grandpa wasn't trying to teach you to swim!" My dad paused, considering his own father and the sometimes tenuous relationship that they had, then returned, "No, I'm pretty sure he was trying to teach me to swim." Then he became kind of quiet and didn't speak much for the remainder of the afternoon.

The point of the story is to note a situation that involves a potentially dangerous act and then examine it from the shore, so to speak. You would likely be concerned if you observed my grandfather rowing the child out into the lake and then tossing him into the water, where he likely flailed and splashed about in an effort to swim, not sink.

You would have very little time to assess the situation for risk but would probably look for contextual clues such as the behavior of the man in the boat, the indication of concern for safety (such as the presence of life jackets or perhaps a rope tied to the boy's leg), and a few historical clues, such as their behavior prior to the incident. Your concerns, and thus your response, would be based upon the context of the situation and not upon psychological information obtained from my grandpa, something you would not have time to gather anyway.

Through assessment of the situation, you are investigating whether or not someone is "posing" a threat, not whether someone "makes" a threat.

In other words, a student who says "I'm going to kill you!" may be expressing his anger to a teacher because he is upset about a poor grade he's received. He may be using bravado to intimidate another student who is posturing to fight or he may be predicting the outcome of an upcoming wrestling match with an opponent. And less likely, he may even be predicting a future attack by making the threat, but the assessment of risk is most accurate when it examines the situation that involves the threatening statement, not the threatening statement isolated from its context. The context of the threat is extremely important, while the words of the threat are less so.

TARGETED AND REACTIVE THREATS AND BEHAVIOR

Examining context is most important when it appears that the behavior or threat is targeted. Targeted threats occur when the attacker considers and selects a particular target prior to attack (Fein et al., 1995). The consideration occurs through the process of an idea with motive, planning, preparation, and eventually action (Calhoun, 1998). Targeted aggression is frequently characterized by minimal or no emotion with a variety of goals such as power, revenge, dominance, money, or sexual gratification.

A far more common type of threat is reactive or affective aggression. Often used as synonymous terms, the two differ in the following ways. Affective aggression is an affectation of rage, power, and/or the capacity to inflict harm, often used to intimidate either before or during an attack. The attacker may be somewhat calculated in the effort but is more often in a reactively aggressive position.

Reactive aggression (impulsive, impromptu) is often temporary, without premeditation, planning, plotting, or specific targeting and is the result of either an imminent threat (real or perceived) or a sort of "last-straw" loss of control resulting from an overwhelming situation. It can be affective and characterized by the emotions of anger and rage or be defensive and fearful. Either way, the goal is to eliminate the threat or the annoyance.

Both aggressive strategies often occur in an emotional or highly aroused state and are responses to perceived challenge, threats, insults, or other affronts (de Becker, 1998; Meloy, 2000). Reactive behavior can be a function within a pattern of socialization as some attackers search for excuses or opportunities to be angry and aggressive, without any predetermined target. And while context is an important feature of assessment in reactive behavior, it is far less complicated than with targeted behavior.

Reid Meloy (1988, 2000, 2006) uses the term "predatory violence" instead of targeted violence and uses the example of cat aggression to illustrate the difference between targeted behavior and reactive (or what he refers to as "affective") behavior. Consider a cat that is cornered by a large dog. The cat is bristled, wild eyed, and in a defensive posture loudly presenting the affectation of tremendous potential violence. If you attempt to rescue this cat, you will likely receive the aggressive treatment intended for the dog. This cat is in a reactive and affective posture.

Consider the same cat stalking a bird on the front lawn. The cat is focused and calm, low to the ground, planning every step and move in order to stay clear of the bird's natural instinct for danger. If you attempt to interfere with this cat's moves, you will likely be ignored or even dismissed, as the cat will move off to a better vantage point that does not involve you. You are not the target, but the bird certainly is.

Dewey Cornell (2004) uses the terms "transient threat" and "substantive threat" to define threats. Transient threats are usually expressed during situations of emotion and upset but lack plans or real intent. Substantive threats occur in a more premeditative manner and involve a plan, intent, and the means by which to act out the threat.

Fredrick Calhoun uses another set of terms to describe the two different types of violent threats (1998). "Hunters" are individuals who are engaged in serious targeted violence. Hunters do not draw unnecessary attention to themselves by making threats, as their intention is to complete their violent plan. "Howlers" are individuals who make repeated threats to harm. These threats may be made in a variety of forms: written, phone, or through a third party. Howlers do not engage in approach behavior, as they have no real intent to carry out their threats. "Howlers don't hunt and Hunters don't howl."

For simplicity, this manual uses the terms "targeted" and "reactive" as the basic descriptors of aggression. Regardless of the terms used, threat assessment is concerned with all manifestations of aggression but, as noted above in the citation from the United States Secret Service, it is most concerned with targeted violence. That is, communication and associated behavior that indicates that a situation poses a threat to a specific target and that there are preparations to attack that target and inflict serious or lethal injury.

While the media continually suggests that targeted violence is a surprise or a result of a person who has "just snapped," the opposite is actually true. Specifically, the following are process steps that have been noted by many experts (Fein et al., 1995; Calhoun, 1998; de Becker, 1998; Meloy, 2000) as indicators of an entry into the continuum of targeted violence.

Step 1. Ideation: Thinking about and considering the idea of acting out violently against specific targets. The ideation involves a motive and often justification. Some common motives are injustice, righteous or vigilante mission, loss, destiny, revenge, recognition, and even the motive of problem solving. Some ideas are discussed openly in an effort to build cause, identify with previous assassins, or other potential accomplices. Often, violence is seen as the only alternative with acceptable consequences.

Ideation can also include weapons fascination or a fixation on anniversaries and other significant dates. Ideation is not always noted in verbal communications but usually can be found in alternative forms of communication such as text messages, emails, or other forms of electronic communication. Journaling, artwork, poetry, story writing, and lyric writing can also express targeted ideation. Even storytelling, fantasy gaming, and violent media immersion can be indicators, especially if they appear to be more of a simulation or rehearsal for the ideas.

Step 2. Planning: Step 2 is the beginning of "attack related behavior" (Fein et al., 1995) or simply put, behavior that supports the threat as something that is being seriously considered or planned or otherwise suggests that the attacker is engaged in activity that facilitates the execution of the threat. Targeted attacks cannot occur without some sort of planning.

Plans may be sophisticated or very simple, but regardless of their level of complexity, once examined, the information suggests notable plans for executing an attack. Such may take the shape of making note of attack process or steps needed for success. Plans may take shape through stalking or approach behavior (practice runs). Target research (suspicious inquiries, information gathering, studying the target and target site), rehearsals, and simulation (practice) are means often used to refine plans.

Step 3. Preparation: Executing a plan requires preparation. Preparations include weapons acquisition, assembling equipment, arranging transportation, observing significant dates, conducting final acts or ceremonial behaviors, costuming, and conducting final personal business (giving away possessions, caring for pets or loved ones). Preparation also includes researching weapons or equipment, practicing with weapons, rehearsals or dry runs (approach behavior), probes of security, prepping the target site, and the use of first-person shooter games or theme-specific movies/entertainment to simulate the act of a targeted assault.

Step 4. Execution or breach: This is the attempt at actually carrying out the targeted act. It may involve eliminating preliminary targets (such as family or police) or using means to gather or disperse crowds in order to better accomplish the goal of completing the targeted act.

PREINCIDENT INDICATORS (OR ANTECEDENTS)

Preincident indicators (Calhoun, 1998; de Becker, 1998) are actions, communications, or circumstances that indicate an individual or group is considering or planning a violent act. The following is a partial list of important factors to consider when assessing the escalation of targeted violence:

- Inappropriate communications
- Threats
- Abnormal/obsessive behavior, depression
- Prior acts of violence
- Keeping a diary
- Purchasing a weapon
- Past violence
- Blaming others and the inability to accept personal responsibility
- Inappropriate reactions
- Sudden irrational beliefs and ideas
- Verbal threats
- Deterioration of personal hygiene
- Romantic obsessions with an uninterested coworker
- Substance abuse
- Little or no social support system
- Conveying violence in journal writing, drawing, or conversation

- Disruptive or aggressive toward people, animals, or property
- Obsession with firearms
- Poor self-esteem
- Anger outbursts
- Constant complaining
- Obsessive behavior
- Stalking
- Rehearsal

ACCELERATORS, TRIGGERS, AND PRECIPITATING EVENTS

Accelerators are destabilizing factors that increase the potential for individuals to resort to violence. These include illness, divorce, financial crisis, decreased or terminated employment, and perceived ongoing abandonment/rejection. Triggers and precipitating events are similar to accelerators but tend to be acute experiences or circumstances that aggravate an individual or group further toward a violent act (Meloy, 2000).

While a situation may be very concerning with an increasing risk, there may be a recent or an upcoming event that will trigger the final decision to go through with an attempted violent act (Mohandie, 2000). The proverbial "straw that breaks the camel's back," such an event may include the loss of a significant inhibitor or the introduction of a new accelerator in a person's life. This event may be viewed by outsiders as insignificant; however, to the person considering a loss of options and the use of violence as a solution, this event may cause the further loss of alternatives or present an intolerable outcome.

Many of these events cause humiliation, shame, and loss of face. A few examples are rejection or the perception of rejection; bullying or ridicule; sudden loss of a significant relationship; failure or loss of privilege due to poor performance; jealousy; or distorted perceptions due to psychosis or other thought disorders (Mohandie, 2000).

INHIBITORS AND STABILIZING FACTORS

So far, this chapter and the last have examined factors that escalate risk or at least indicate that a concern should be further examined. Assessment must also look at protective factors that "inhibit" or decrease risk and slow down or even stop the escalation to targeted violence. According to Gavin de Becker (1998), inhibitors are positive factors that are present in a potential attacker's life that would inhibit him or her from acting in a violent manner.

Mohandie (2000) describes stabilizing factors as strengths that contribute to restrain impulses and improve prosocial problem solving. Mohandie suggests that stabilizers are often "risk factors in reverse." The following is not a complete list of stabilizers, but an example of factors that may be important features to identify, maintain, or even add to a situation in an effort to manage it safely. Of course, each set of circumstances is unique, and what may be an inhibitor in one situation may, as Mohandie has suggested, become an aggravator or trigger in another (2000).

- Employment or academic success
- Finances and resources
- Health and treatment options
- Residence
- Spirituality
- Prosocial friends, peer support
- Family, siblings, children
- Optimistic outlook for future or identified prosocial goals
- Coping skills, easygoing disposition, friendly attitude
- Emotional resiliency
- Sports, music, art, theater, extracurricular activities, scouts, religious clubs, school politics, and so on
- Work or a job
- Extended family with concerned support
- Structure and stability
- Dignity, even pride
- Peer respect or favorable reputation
- Routine and constructive scheduled activity
- Pets

THE JACA ELEMENTS
(AN ACRONYM FOR QUICK ASSESSMENT)

In his book *The Gift of Fear* (1998), Gavin de Becker published the acronym JACA as a mnemonic device for remembering key aspects to the assessment of risk (1998). The four risk factors are foundational within the work of threat assessment.

- *J* is for justification: Does the person feel justified in using violence? Common justifications include taking the moral high ground, righteous indignation, or revenge and payback (such as "an eye for an eye").

- *A* is for alternatives: Does the person perceive any available alternatives to the use of violence? Since all behavior including violence has a purpose, it is advantageous to know the goal or motive of the person. Providing alternatives is an effective management tool. Sometimes an alternative is as simple as an available complaint process, appeal, or identifiable contact person who will listen, mentor, or provide a nondefensive ear.
- *C* is for consequences: How does the person perceive the consequences associated with the use of violence? Before resorting to targeted violence, a person will weigh the consequences of a violent act. Most of the time, the consequences will be intolerable. When the consequences are perceived as acceptable or favorable, violence is likely.
- *A* is for ability: Does the person believe he can successfully commit the act of violence? People who have successfully used violence in the past have a higher perception of their ability to be successful in their use of violence. Ability is a perception in the perpetrator's mind and may not be an accurate measurement of intellect or skill. In other words, if someone thinks they are capable of a complex plan of attack, they may attempt the attack regardless of their actual intellectual limitation or skills. While the attack may not be successful, the attempt would likely lead to an unfortunate outcome.

DYNAMICS OF FOUR TYPES OF CONCERNING YOUTH AGGRESSION

Typical youth aggression, by the standards of this book, is not particularly concerning and is thus not addressed below. "Typical" is defined as occasional fighting or hostility (not resulting in serious injury) that is a result of conflict that is within the range of usual youth life experience. Of concern, however, are the following:

1. Vengeance or revenge: Threats or acts of aggressive vengeance are often made as a reaction to being hurt, challenged, or wronged in some way. As such, they are frequently reactive in nature and serve as an affectation of strength and justice. Occasionally, however, threats of revenge can be made in the form of a veiled prediction of future violence and may well indicate a predatory and thus targeted plan to cause harm. Almost all targeted school violence has been driven by vengeance as a primary or partial feature of the motive. Revengeful aggression can be both reactive and targeted but is more frequently reactive.
2. Troubled or disturbed youth: Students with mental disabilities, severe emotional distress, or profound mood disturbances often struggle internally

because of ongoing anxiety and disruption. As a result, they can be irritable, short fused, and have a low reserve of coping skills. They can also be aggressive and combative, but almost always as a reactionary defense strategy or an affectation of bravado that can be very intimidating to others. In order to engage in a targeted or predatory process of aggression, a student must be capable of organizing, planning, and being carefully patient enough to await opportunity; therefore, most impulsive or emotionally distressed students tend to lack the follow-through necessary to successfully target another student for a sustained length of time. Nevertheless, a disorganized and extremely troubled student should not be underestimated when it comes to being capable of targeted violence, especially if given a justifiable motive and circumstances.

3. Gang: Gang aggression can be both reactive and targeted. Drive-by shootings or approaching a rival gang with the anticipation of engaging them in a fight are examples of targeted acts, while engaging a rival gang in a fight as a reaction to a surprise crossing of paths at the wrong time is an example of a reactive event.

4. Love/relationship: Relationship aggression often has similar dynamics to domestic violence within the married adult population. Students engaged in romantic relationships will sometimes use the same threats of aggression or hurtful behavior as a means of controlling their boyfriend or girlfriend. That aggression can appear reactive at first, especially if it is a response to an upsetting breakup or change of relationship status, but the aggression can also be a planned, calculated, and targeted use of rage (or what appears to be reactive anger) to impose their will and wants. This is addressed further in chapter 11, under the subtitle of Domestic Violence.

In summary, the concepts presented within this chapter are basic to a foundational understanding of threat assessment. With the right motive, justification, and circumstance, absent stabilizing factors, every human being is capable of being violent (de Becker, 1998). Human beings are wired for aggression. The ability to defend one's self, family, and community is an important part of our history, evolution, and socialization.

James Cawood (who is cited throughout this book under the reference Corcoran and Cawood, 2003) has noted that aggressive behavior is a feature possessed by all people capable of basic functioning, regardless of their age, development, or cognitive ability. The key to threat assessment is determining if a circumstance is such that a particular person or group can justify the use of violence to solve a particular problem, address a threat, or defend an interest. In other words, threat assessment is determining the factors necessary for an individual or group to act out.

The most effective manner in which to do this is through a collaborative or teaming effort (involving professionals from education, law enforcement, mental health, and others as needed) that determines facts, examines circumstances, takes the needed immediate action necessary to ensure safety, then follows up with more assessment and a longer-term management plan. This can be done through a combined use of protocols specific to each discipline but designed for the use of assessing threat (such as those provided within this manual) or compiling information through the use of other types of assessment tools, computer surveys, or questionnaires.

Regardless of how the information is gathered, the important feature of the assessment is that the risk factors are examined and determined through team investigation, discussion, and decision making and not through a quantifiable questionnaire or a set of questions that load into a profile or compartmentalized and predetermined result.

Finally, once the information is assessed and risk is determined and addressed, it is important to avoid making future predictions or using labels to describe individuals. Threat assessment is addressing situations that are dangerous—situations that may contain one or more individuals who pose a danger to others but who are not necessarily dangerous individuals.

By addressing the situation, the process focuses on decreasing aggravators and accelerators, adding inhibitors and stabilizing factors, and changing the circumstantial issues that are increasing the risk of violence. This can be done at a considerably faster pace than a mental health evaluation, personality profile, or psychiatric evaluation of the individual and without the need to make predictive statements. It can be done by simply defining the risk and then addressing the risk with an appropriate management strategy.

With the basic concepts in mind, take a moment to review the six scenarios presented at the beginning of this chapter and see if your concerns have changed. As you read through them, make note of information that is missing or needs to be further investigated. Keep this in mind as you read the following chapters outlining application and protocol.

System, Team Dynamics, and Applications of Student Threat Assessment

Chapter Five

Level 1 (Site-Based Assessment)

John Van Dreal

The previous chapters have reviewed the research, recommendations, and operational concepts suggested by national as well as regional experts. This chapter begins the application of that material into a system administered through community support and school district commitment.

As previously noted, it is a two-tiered process involving a site-based assessment (called a Level 1) with the application of supervision and intervention strategies followed by a community-based assessment (called a Level 2) when needed (see appendix 1 A). The system utilizes a centralized reporting structure at both site and community levels and examines threats or implied threats of aggression, moving from the assessment of threat to the management of threat (at both levels) using strategies that reasonably and prudently address the risk factors and situational variables elevating the risk.

It also provides for ongoing follow-up and reassessment as the identified risk factors are adjusted to the supervision and intervention. The system is administered and maintained through multidisciplinary and multiagency collaboration with a strong focus on changing the circumstances that aggravate and elevate the potential for aggression. As such, it operates without the use of labels, myths, profiling, and overreaction.

The system is engaged at Level 1 when a threat or threatening situation is detected or suspected. The definition of a threat, simply stated, is the intention to commit harm to a target or be a menace or source of danger to a target. Within this protocol, "target" refers to another human being but certainly leaves open the possibility of an assessment of any situation that causes concern or suggests the possibility of an aggressive outcome.

An implied threat or act of aggression occurs when a person (in this system, a student or group of students) engages in or considers aggression directed

at another person or persons. The system is *not* to be used for students who
are suicidal, acting out sexually, or setting fires, unless they are doing so in
combination with or as a function of an act of extreme aggression intending
severe or lethal injury to others.

The system has three tracks. The first and second tracks are noted in
figure 5.1. The first is protective response when imminent danger exists. In
this situation, an imminent threat warrants immediate security and response
and law enforcement is notified (911) followed by the appropriate district
offices such as central administration and security. (In other words, initiate a
protective response using school district guidelines.) The second is done by
law enforcement when criminal investigation is warranted.

The third track is assessment (Level 1) and is initiated by the administrator
with consultation from another member of the site team (see figure 5.2). The
site team is composed of an administrator, school counselor, and school resource officer (SRO) trained in the use of the Level 1 process and the Level 1

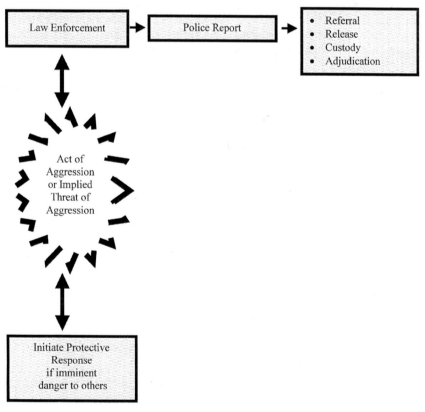

Figure 5.1

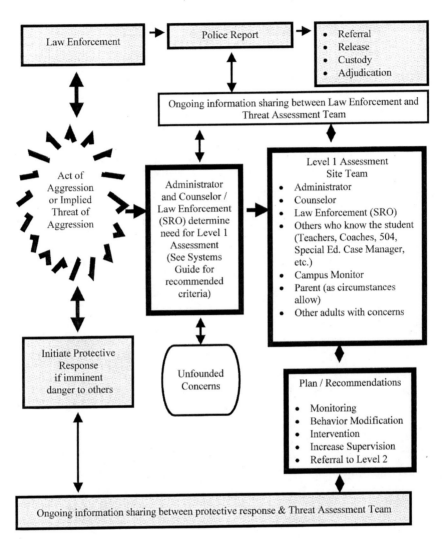

Figure 5.2

Assessment Protocol (see appendix 1 B, appendix 1 B.1, and description/ instructions noted below).

If the school site does not have a counselor or SRO as assigned staff, teachers or other support staff can be included as team members if trained in the use of the protocol. Another option may be to use neighboring school staff and/or the consultation of local mental health agencies and local law enforcement through an agreement of cooperation and support.

LEVEL 1 (SITE TEAM) ASSESSMENT

Level 1 site team members can be trained using this chapter as a guide (see also appendix 1 C) combined with the noted forms and flow charts from the appendix.

The Level 1 Assessment Protocol (appendix 1 B) is designed for investigation and documentation of concerns about dangerous student activities, behaviors, ideation, and/or statements. A direct threat (expressed or acted out) does not have to be clearly indicated in order to proceed with a Level 1 assessment. Site teams are encouraged to use the Level 1 assessment to address concerns and document their review of potential danger or safety issues, even if dismissed as minor or unlikely.

The Level 1 assessment process can be used as a reasonably short (twenty- to thirty-minute) review or a more extensive and lengthy assessment, depending upon the circumstances. Furthermore, the Level 1 found in appendix 1 B is the recommended protocol for documenting concerns, interventions, and actions; however, if a school or district is short on staffing resources and training, a shorter version containing only the questions identified in the Safe School Initiative may be used as a quick assessment tool prior to referral for further assessment or assistance from a Level 2 team (see appendix 1 B.2).

The following are guidelines for considering a Level 1 assessment (that utilizes the Level 1 protocol from appendix 1 B):

- Threat or aggression is specific to identified target with motive and plan.
- Threat or aggression is causing considerable fear or disruption to activity.
- There is continued intent to carry out threat.
- There is a history of threats or moderate to extreme aggression.
- Staff, parent, or student perceives threatening circumstances.
- Administrator is unable to determine if a situation poses a risk to school personnel or the community.

The results of the Level 1 assessment do not predict future aggression nor are they a foolproof method of assessing an individual's or group's risk of harm to others. The questions that follow are not a checklist that can be quantified. They are a guide designed to assist in the investigation of potential danger (to identify circumstances and variables that may increase risk for potential youth aggression) and to assist the school staff in developing a management plan. Furthermore, as circumstances change, so too does risk potential; therefore, when doing the follow-up review after assessments, be mindful of the impact of supervision, intervention, and the passage of time.

To Conduct a Level 1 Assessment:

A. Schedule assessment as soon as the site team can assemble. Make sure all students/staff are safe. If necessary take appropriate precautions such as detaining the student and restricting access to coats, backpacks, lockers, and so on. If imminent danger exists, call law enforcement and district-level office and follow district safety guidelines (see figures 5.1 and 5.2). Prepare the Level 1 Assessment Protocol (appendix 1 B) noted above and in item E below.

Administrator and/or police officer (if appropriate) interview the student or students of concern prior to the assessment meeting and note their version of the reported threat, the situation, communications, behavior relating to a possible attack, motives, access to weaponry, accelerating factors, and protective supports.

B. Invite staff who know the student(s) well to attend the assessment meeting. Consider English, humanities, and art teachers who have information from writings or creative work, campus monitor(s), and education case managers if the student is on an IEP (Individual Education Plan) or 504 plan (Section 504 of the Rehabilitation Act of 1973 prohibits discrimination against persons with disabilities). The primary questions from Level 1 are condensed into a short teacher questionnaire (see appendix 1 D) and are available for education staff to complete if they are unable to attend the scheduled assessment. Responses from the teacher questionnaire should be transferred to the Level 1 protocol using the corresponding item numbers located in parentheses at the end of each question.

C. Also include community agency case managers if the student is adjudicated or a ward of the court.

D. The parent/guardian should be notified that the assessment will be taking place and invited to attend if the administrator determines that their participation will be constructive to the assessment process. The site team may elect to complete the assessment without notification and/or inclusion of the parent if it is determined that the participation of the parent would compromise the process and mislead conclusions or safety decisions.

Documentation for parental notification is on the Level 1 assessment. If parent or guardian does not attend the meeting, the primary questions are condensed into a short parent questionnaire (see appendix 1 E) and are available to complete by phone or personal interview (counselor or administrator completes the questionnaire by interviewing parent or guardian). Responses from the parent questionnaire should be transferred to the Level 1 protocol using the corresponding item numbers located in parentheses at the end of each question.

E. With administrative leadership and through team discussion and information gathering (including information from the interview conducted with the student/s of concern and the information transferred from the parent questionnaire and any teacher questionnaires if obtained), conduct the Level 1 assessment using the Level 1 protocol as the primary documentation.

The Level 1 protocol includes step-by-step directions, demographics, assessment questions, and intervention ideas to address risk factors and supervision strategies to address management needs. It also provides the recommended criteria for considering further assessment through the Level 2 process.

F. Step 3 of the Level 1 protocol provides twenty questions that are listed as abbreviated versions of the risk factors noted in the research in chapter 3. The Level 1 Protocol Companion (appendix 1 F) is an explanatory supplement to be used along with the questions on the Level 1 protocol. The Level 1 questions and the companion's explanations are summarized as follows.

1. Define threats or dangerous situation using the aggression continuum (see figure 4.1 in chapter 4). Is aggression mild (a high-frequency but low-impact behavior such as light hitting, kicking, or biting); moderate (infrequent but with greater impact in injury such as fistfighting); or extreme (rare, but impact is serious or even lethal injury such as beating, raping, stabbing, shooting, or bombing)?

   This question asks for a clarification of the threat. Note the location of the threat, behavior, or dangerous situation on the continuum illustrated in figure 4.1. Note that there is a change within the continuum from mild aggression (nonserious or nonlethal injury) to extreme aggression or what is sometimes termed as violence (serious or lethal injury).

   Also, while there is a suggested progression of behavior from mild to extreme, the listed examples serve only as illustration and are not necessarily locked into their position within the continuum. In other words, hitting can be a mild, moderate, or even extreme form of aggression, depending upon the intention or the outcome of harm.

2. Have there been any communications suggesting a potential attack or act of moderate to extreme aggression (direct threats, specific references, veiled threats, or vague warnings)?

   This question addresses the type of communication indicating a threat. Threats are sometimes made directly in verbal communication, art, email, Internet use, written language exercises, and any other medium of communication. They can also be made by indirect, veiled, or casual references to possible harmful events, ominous warnings, or references to previously occurring violent events such as school shootings.

A threat does not have to be specifically stated to be of concern, nor does it have to be stated or implied within the school setting.

3. Are there indications of a plan, feasible process, or clear intention to harm others?

   This question addresses attack-related behavior. Threatening language is just language without related behavior or intent. Many threats are not stated with language but are indicated by vague references combined with related behavior. Attack-related behavior may be, but is not limited to, the following:

   • A plan (complex or simple) to carry out a targeted act of violence against a specific individual, group, or student body. Such a plan would have a sequence of actions necessary for its success and almost always requires a motive. The more plausible and detailed the plan, the greater the risk.
   • The acquisition of a weapon, the attempted acquisition of a weapon, or research about how to acquire a weapon. (If the threat is the use of physical force to the point of serious or lethal injury, then the physical force is the weapon.)
   • The rehearsal of the event or a similar event. Rehearsal is like simulation or practice. Rehearsal or simulation is often necessary before a targeted event can be completely planned and carried out. Rehearsal can be indicated through art, fantasy games, writing or film projects, the use of movies or Internet sites that have themes and sequences of targeted violence that allow the simulation of targeted and violent acts, or through first-person shooter video games that also allow for simulation of sequential and violent acts. However, the use of such games or movies as entertainment does not lead students to act out violently. Their use is only attack-related behavior when it becomes rehearsal or simulation and practice.
   • Scheduling an attack. Scheduling the act is sometime indicated through communication or actually noted in clear detail. Sometimes the schedule is flexible, awaiting a triggering event (teasing, rejection, loss) that further justifies the violence and locks it in as the only solution.

4. Are there indications of suicidal ideation, intent, or planning?

   This question examines the presence or history of suicidal ideas, gestures, references, and intent. The wish to die, be killed, or commit suicide combined with a threat to harm others increases risk, especially if the self-destructive behavior is the last part of a plan to harm others and carry out revenge or justice.

5. Are there indications of a specific target(s) or focus of aggression?

   This question examines the focus of the aggressive ideation. Is there an ongoing consideration or focus on a particular person, group, or student body? If the situation is absent a notable target, it is likely a situation that revolves around reactive aggression, used as a means to bully, intimidate, confront, or defend interests and wants.

6. Are there indications of a weapons choice and availability?

   This question examines a primary concern; however, it is important to remember that even if weapons are not available within the home, they are frequently available within the community.

7. Are there indications of a focused or unusual interest in acts of violence, previous school attacks or attackers, weaponry or antisocial characters, notorious criminals, murderers, or gangs (historical or fictional)?

   This question is somewhat complicated. What may be inappropriate to some may still be within the normal scope of age, cultural, or developmental range for others. The question is similar to #3, as it examines whether the interest is a curiosity, a fascination, or a sort of admiration for the antisocial character as role model and example of how to justify violence as problem solving.

8. Are there indications of a motive or goal for aggressive behavior or a lethal attack?

   This question pairs with #5. If there is a focus on a specific target or targets, then there is very likely a motive. While there can certainly be many motives for acting out violently, the most common is the need to establish or reestablish control as indicated by revenge or vendetta for lost love or humiliation and the desire to prove bravery after making a threat or taking a dare.

   If the situation is absent a motive, then it may revolve around reactive aggression or the affectation of rage. Reactive aggressive talk often has triggers that agitate the situation rapidly. Such triggers are usually not motives but should still be identified in order to avoid or eliminate them in the future.

9. Are there indications of hopeless, stressed, overwhelming, victimized, or desperate situations (real or perceived)?

   This question examines another primary concern. As students lose hope of resolving stressful or overwhelming situations through acceptable social or coping skills, they are more likely to engage desperate solutions and last-ditch efforts to take control. It is important to note that the point of this question is to examine the perception of the person or party you are concerned with, not necessarily what is realistically observed or known by others (staff, parents, other students, or the community).

10. Are there indications of capacity or ability to carry out an act of targeted/planned violence?

This question examines the feasibility or possibility of a planned and carried-out threat, based upon the organizational, cognitive, or adaptive capacity of the person or party of concern. If someone is making fairly exaggerated or complex threats but is unable to organize due to supervision, cognitive ability, or overall functioning, then the feasibility decreases.

11. Are beliefs or ideas irrational or a feature of a mental health disorder (paranoid, obsessive, a feature of a disability)? Are values, beliefs, or ideas socially maladjusted (sees aggression as a justifiable method of problem solving and accepts consequences)?

This question examines connections between threats and disability. Threatening talk as a feature of mental illness is often grandiose or implausible and is usually disconnected from attack-related behavior (see question #3), targeted behavior (see question #5), and even clear motive (see question #8). Attack-related behavior, if it exists, is more quickly determined. Typically, threats that are made and are features of disabilities are less concerning than those that are made or implied with thoughtful and sober consideration that follows a process of reason and justification.

12. Are actions and behaviors consistent with any threatening communications?

This question examines the relationship between communicated threats or implications of threat and the behavior that accompanies the communication. If threats are made but there is an absence of attack-related behaviors, motives, or a specific target(s) consistent with that threat, then risk decreases. Many threats that lack attack-related behavior, a target, or motive are likely to be a means of communicating dissatisfaction, attention seeking, expressing anger, releasing stress, or even an affectation of strength or power (bravado).

13. Are caregivers, peers, and/or staff concerned about potential for violent behavior?

This question examines the perceptions and opinions of others regarding the person or party of concern and the concerning situation that exists. Concerns may range from an odd discomfort to a complete list of reasons why caution should be taken. If violence is being considered or planned, it is difficult to hide the indicators. In fact, sometimes little care is actually taken to hide the intentions and, while there may be little to no documentation of past behavioral issues, there may likely be several people who have been or are currently concerned.

14. Are there trusting, successful relationships with one or more responsible adults?

This question examines the depth of relationships with prosocial adults. The greater and healthier the connection with teachers, coaches, parents, administrators, church leaders, and so on, the less chance there is of wanting to disappoint or hurt them. The situation involving a marginalized student who lacks any connection to adults is often one of greater risk, as there is less to lose by acting out.

This is one of the most important questions and indicators of need on the Level 1 protocol. If a student or group of students lacks connection to prosocial adults and is also marginalized within the student population, then intervention and connection are strongly indicated.

15. What aggravating factors—circumstances, events, or triggers—increase or agitate the likelihood of an aggressive attack?

This question examines the obvious. If you can identify the situations that agitate or trigger aggressive thinking, threats, and behavior, you can intervene and decrease the chance of an aggressive incident.

16. What circumstances, events, or inhibitors decrease the likelihood of an aggressive attack?

This question is similar to #15 but examines the opposite. Identify and increase actions, events, interests, relationships, goals, activities, memberships, and so on that promote responsible and accountable prosocial behavior and you can decrease the chance of an aggressive incident. The situation that lacks any inhibitors is one of greater risk, as there is little to lose by acting out and little to motivate healthy solutions.

17. Are there indications that peer group reinforces delinquent thinking? What are relationship dynamics (leader, follower, victim, outcast, marginalized, disconnected, etc.)?

This question examines peer relationships, marginalization, and accepted delinquent thinking that may support using violence as a solution. Risk increases if a situation lacks positive social connection, accountability, and inhibitors but is filled with antisocial thinking about entitlement, revenge, and the use of violence as an acceptable means of solving problems.

18. Is there a history of school, behavioral, drug/alcohol, or developmental issues?

This question examines issues that are related to vulnerability and coping skills but are not necessarily directly related to targeted or planned violence. Risk increases considerably as coping strategies are limited.

19. Are there mental health issues?

    This question is similar to question #18 in that it examines an issue that may indicate a poor reserve of coping strategies and a lack of emotional resiliency.

20. Other concerns:

    This is an open question. Remember that Level 1 is not a quantifiable questionnaire or a fixed checklist. It is intended as a set of pertinent questions that outline an examination of concerns and potential risk.

G. Use the supervision strategies and interventions noted below (also suggested in step 4 of the Level 1 protocol, appendix 1 B) to address the concerns and aggravating factors identified through the above-noted questions (step 3 of the Level 1 protocol). The following examples are resources and options available within the Salem-Keizer School District in Salem, Oregon.

Individual Options:

- Intended victim warned—parent/guardian notified (see notification form, appendix 1 G)
- Protective response initiated by security department
- Individual accountability plan
- Suicide assessment initiated on (use district suicide protocol)
- No-harm contract
- Student will self-manage. Describe: _____.

School Options:

- Review educational plan
- Specialized class options
- Travel card and time accountability
- Social skill–building programs
- Increase supervision in following settings: _____
- Modifications of daily schedule/late arrival/early dismissal
- Alert staff and teachers on need-to-know basis
- Decrease or eliminate pass time or unsupervised time
- Random check of backpack, locker, pocket, purse, and so on
- Assign identified staff to build trusting relationship through check-in or mentorship: administrator; mentor; child development specialist/counselor; school resource officer; teacher; other: _____.
- Provide means by which student may safely report and discuss thoughts or intentions to harm others and receive appropriate intervention

- Other interventions or supervision strategies that will directly address the triggers and agitators identified in step 3
- Identify and further develop activities, relationships, or experiences of value that inhibit possibility of acting out
- CDS/school counselor or prevention intervention resource specialist (PIRS) intervention
- Referral to appropriate school team to consider alternative placement
- Home supervision pending further assessment
- Increased supervision in the following settings: _____.
- Referral to appropriate special education team to consider psychoeducational evaluation/special education (*Note:* If student is on IEP/504 plan, any change in placement or special education services must be done through special education team process or 504 team process.)
- Assessment or behavior team referral (*Note:* Must be done through special education team process.)

Family/Home Options:

- Strategize safety options/planning
- Increase supervision
- Safety-proof home
- Review and pursue crisis and/or mental health services

Community Options:

- Referral to YST
- Student will self-manage. Describe: _____.
- Mental health evaluation
- Anger management programs
- Alcohol/drug evaluation
- Parenting programs
- Mentoring programs
- Notify probation/parole officer
- Faith community programs
- Foster positive community activities, interests
- Referral to Level 2 (community-level assessment): Contact STAT if in-depth assessment and assistance is needed (see figure 5.3). The following criteria are suggested to assist Level 1 teams as they consider a referral for a Level 2 assessment (see appendix 1 B, Level 1 protocol, step 5):

    1. Student brought gun to school or attempted to acquire gun with possible intent to harm others.

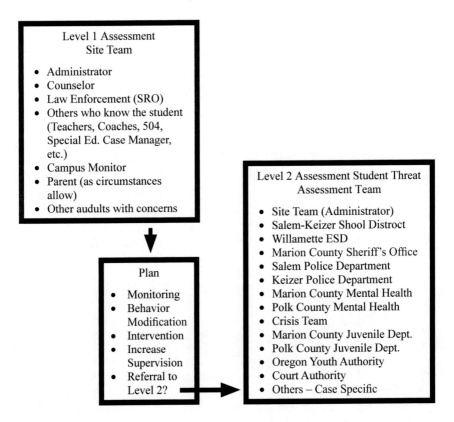

Figure 5.3

2. The Level 1 team is unable to confidently answer items on Level 1 protocol.
3. Safety concerns are significant and beyond site team's ability to supervise and secure within the building.
4. Exploration of community resources is needed to assist in supervision.

Once referred, STAT will schedule the Level 2 investigation team as well as other professionals and key sources of information (such as juvenile probation officers, state caseworkers, therapists, etc.). Step 5 on the Level 1 protocol further notes the information necessary to determine those who need to attend the Level 2 investigation. (The system's Level 2 process will be reviewed in the following chapter.)

H. To complete the Level 1 process, fax a copy of Level 1 parent and teacher questionnaires if obtained and incident report if written to district resources noted in step 6 on the Level 1 protocol.

I. Notify the parents/guardians of any identified potential targets or victims using the notification log (appendix 1 G) and the notification letter (appendix 1 H). The notification call is to be done within twelve hours; notification letter sent within twenty-four hours. (See Oregon Revised Statute 339.225.) Then consider completing a Plan to Protect Targeted or Victimized Student (appendix 1 I), taking into consideration concerns identified by the targeted student and his or her parents/guardians.

J. Maintain two copies of Level 1 protocols, one in a letter-size manila envelope marked "Confidential" and placed in the student's regular academic or cumulative file and a second copy as the administrator's or counselor's working file (available to or copies also to counselors and SROs). Update the clerical demographic records (such as SASI or other district records) to note the presence of a confidential envelope.

K. If the case was referred for a Level 2 assessment, place one copy of the Level 2 summary in the confidential envelope and a second copy in the administrator's working file along with the Level 1.

L. The case is tracked and managed by the school administrator. Schedule follow-up dates for the review of the supervision plan and monitor the risk factors as needed.

To summarize, this system relies on a strong Level 1 process that is based upon the assessment of available information with accompanying supervision strategies drawn from available resources. Its primary function is to assess risk and search out and apply inhibiting factors that reduce that risk. The system is not a process for the prediction of future acts or a means by which to label or profile a student.

The following chapter will review STAT (the community team) and the Level 2 process.

Chapter Six

Level 2 (Community-Based Assessment) Overview

John Van Dreal

The previous chapter reviewed the Level 1 process. The next three chapters (6 through 8) review the Level 2 (or community team) process. Comprehension of the contents and information in these chapters is reliant upon a strong understanding of the principles and research provided in previous chapters. While the perusal of this chapter is recommended for anyone participating in the system, it is primarily written for those who will be engaged in threat assessment at participation levels beyond the Level 1 assessment.

To review, the system examines situations that pose a threat of extreme aggression (violence) and applies management strategies to decrease the risk of a violent outcome. The system does not use labels, profiling, or future predictions or depend upon a zero-tolerance mindset. It is a two-tier system with a site-based component, called a Level 1, and a community-based component called a Level 2 (see figure 6.1 for specific agencies as example).

The Level 2 team or student threat assessment team (STAT) is composed of members from educational districts and institutions, law enforcement, public mental health, juvenile justice, the state youth authority, and the courts. A genuine collaboration of youth-serving agencies (see figure 6.1), it is a community-based consultation team that assesses situations of risk for violence and collaborates on solutions, resource exploration, and supervision planning with schools or other member organizations.

The team does not mandate interventions and does not have the authority to bypass or override the policy or procedure of any agency or institution (this includes the IEP process for placement in special education.) While the Level 2 team shares in the responsibility of school and community safety, the school or agency Level 1 team maintains the case management, authority, and responsibility for final decisions about management, intervention, and supervision.

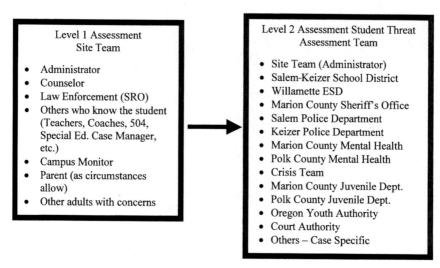

Figure 6.1

The Level 1 site team administrator may request a Level 2 assessment after reviewing the referral guidelines noted in figure 6.2, in chapter 5, or in the Level 1 protocol, step 5 (see appendix 1 B). The dispatch or coordinator of the Level 2 team may use the following questions to clarify the need for further assessment (see appendix 2 A); however, if the Level 2 team has enough time and resources, it is always best to proceed with further assessment as requested:

1. Where is the student on the aggression continuum?
2. What kind of communication has the student/students made regarding their intention to harm others? Are the communications statements of anger such as "I'm going to kill you..." or are they expressions that involve details of planning or ongoing consideration of an attack?
3. Are there any indications of a plan, feasible process, or clear intention to harm others? Examples are acquiring weapons, rehearsing the attack, simulation of the attack, preparations, and/or scheduling the event? Does the behavior match the threat?
4. Is the threat target-specific?
5. Are weapons or means available to carry out the threat?
6. Does the student think that he or she is out of alternatives? For example, if the student is still willing to speak with the school counselor, he or she is *not* out of alternatives. Does the student view violence as an acceptable method of solving problems?
7. Is there a motive?
8. Is the student willing to accept the consequences of carrying out the threat?

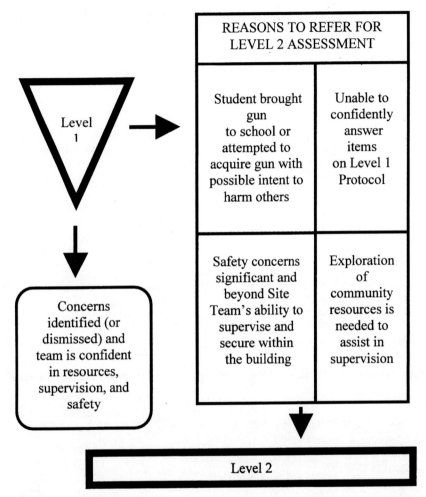

Figure 6.2

A Level 2 assessment is conducted primarily at the school site by an investigative team representing the entire Level 2 team membership or STAT. The investigative team is composed of three primary members: a school psychologist or education specialist trained in threat assessment, a mental health worker, and a law enforcement threat assessment specialist (see figure 6.3). Other members of STAT may also be included in the investigative team as appropriate to the case (such as a juvenile probation counselor, Oregon Youth Authority counselor, or a Child Protective Services case manager).

The three primary members of the investigative team complete their investigation through the use of a protocol reflecting their professional perspective

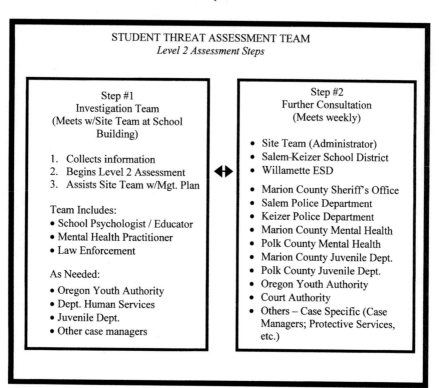

Figure 6.3

but focusing on threat assessment. (Chapter 7 will further detail the investigative team process and protocols.)

After the investigative team completes their assessment and consults on management strategies, the case is scheduled for further Level 2 review and advisement with the entire STAT noted above. A member of the Level 1 site team (the administrator in most cases) will also attend the Level 2 STAT staffing. STAT consultation will further advise on violence risk, management and intervention strategies, and community resources and will continue to support school and other agency professionals as they use STAT recommendations to manage the case.

The Level 2 STAT meets weekly (or more often if needed) and reviews cases using the following format:

• *Up to 10 minutes*: Case manager (school administrator/counselor, agency caseworker, and/or police officer) reviews threat or incident, concerns, current supervision and intervention, and outcomes of current supervision and intervention.

- *Up to 15 minutes*: STAT investigative team (Level 2) presents results of assessment.
- *Up to 20 minutes*: STAT conducts further assessment, consults on supervision strategies, and explores community resources.

Once a student is staffed, case management continues at the school site by the building administrator and is reviewed on a schedule determined at the time of the assessment or as needed if the situation escalates. Members of STAT provide follow-up and consultation as circumstances change and/or supervision needs increase. Because the threat and situation is considered fluid and varies with intervention and supervision changes, the case may be reviewed and reassessed at any time upon the request of the site team.

A Level 2 assessment summary documenting the risk factors and supervision strategies is written by the investigative team leader (usually the school psychologist or education specialist) and provided to the site team case manager (see appendix 2 B for example). Copies of all threat assessment documentation are to be maintained in the confidential envelope located in the student cumulative file.

Any electronic or written demographic record (such as SASI) should be updated to note the presence of a confidential envelope. The Level 2 investigative team leader should also keep copies of documentation, along with investigation notes, in a personal file or a file maintained as a part of a law enforcement unit record (further defined in chapter 8).

As an overview, this chapter outlined the Level 2 process within the system. The following two chapters divide the Level 2 process into two components—the investigative team and the operations of the full community team.

Chapter Seven

Level 2 Investigation Team

John Van Dreal, Allan Rainwater, Dave Okada

As noted in chapter 6, the investigative team conducts the bulk of the Level 2 investigation through meetings and interviews with school staff, parents, and other sources of information (this is most easily done in one meeting that includes all of the sources and information). Following the recommendations from the studies noted in chapter 3, the team members comprise education, mental health, and law enforcement.

Members are trained in threat assessment, threat management, and appropriate-resource identification. As a threat assessment investigation team, they represent the entire community team (STAT) and maintain ongoing communication and consultation as needed (see figure 7.1, an example of the Oregon Mid-Valley team membership). Once the primary portion of the investigation is complete and initial safety and management strategies are offered, the case is moved to the regularly scheduled STAT meeting as outlined in chapter 6. (The STAT meeting schedule and protocol is further outlined in chapter 8.) Each member of the investigation team conducts their threat assessment using an investigation protocol created from their particular professional perspective (education, mental health, or law enforcement). The following are the perspectives and protocol assessment questions.

EDUCATION

The majority of threat assessments are done through or within the schools. In fact, even when initiated through the juvenile department or another STAT agency, the bulk of the work and investigation usually takes place using school resources and information. Furthermore, the schools house and supervise youth for a large portion of their waking day and thus should take

```
┌──────────────────────────────────────────────────────┐
│                  Site Team completed the              │
│                    Level 1 Assessment                 │
│      and requests further investigation and/or consultation │
│                     from STAT (Level 2)               │
└──────────────────────────────────────────────────────┘
```

┌───┐
│   STUDENT THREAT ASSESSMENT TEAM   │
│   *Level 2 Assessment Steps*   │
│   │
│ ┌──────────────────────────┐   ┌─────────────────────────┐ │
│ │   Step #1   │   │   Step #2   │ │
│ │   Investigation Team   │   │   Further Consultation │ │
│ │ (Meets w/Site Team at School │   │   (Meets weekly)   │ │
│ │   Building)   │   │   │ │
│ │   │   │ • Site Team (Administrator) │
│ │ 1. Collects information │   │ • Salem-Keizer School District │
│ │ 2. Begins Level 2 Assessment │   │ • Willamette ESD   │ │
│ │ 3. Assists Site Team w/Mgt. Plan │ │ • Marion County Sheriff's Office │
│ │   │   │ • Salem Police Department │
│ │ Team Includes: │   │ • Keizer Police Department │
│ │ • School Psychologist / Educator │ │ • Marion County Mental Health │
│ │ • Mental Health Practitioner │   │ • Polk County Mental Health │
│ │ • Law Enforcement   │   │ • Marion County Juvenile Dept. │
│ │   │   │ • Polk County Juvenile Dept. │
│ │ As Needed: │   │ • Oregon Youth Authority │
│ │ • Oregon Youth Authority │   │ • Court Authority   │ │
│ │ • Dept. Human Services │   │ • Others – Case Specific (Case │
│ │ • Juvenile Dept.   │   │   Managers; Protective Services, │
│ │ • Other case managers   │   │   etc.)   │ │
│ └──────────────────────────┘   └─────────────────────────┘ │
└───┘

Figure 7.1

the lead in organizing and implementing the threat assessment system. One
feature of this role is the leadership of the Level 2 investigative team.

The educator most qualified to provide the leadership is a licensed (or certified) professional, trained in threat assessment, with a strong understanding
of psychoeducational assessment, the details and rules of special education
protocol, clinical and psychological diagnostics, school discipline code,
and some sense of school administrative rules and procedures. The position
should be filled by someone who has well-established and positive relationships with other educators and a confidence and ability to continue ongoing
communication, follow-up, and reporting.

The lead position is also responsible for interpreting the education discipline's vocabulary, acronyms, mandates, rules, and nomenclature to the other members of the team. In most districts, the school psychologist is best suited to fit this description, although some districts have used a school social worker, behavior specialist, special education administrator, or other licensed educator with the training and education that meets the above specifications.

The education member leading the investigation team must offer the team a strong understanding of school systems, rules, and even the politics that can be subtext to some of the decisions or resource restrictions. Furthermore, the education member must have a strong understanding of the limitations of the school district. This perspective, combined with an understanding of educational and clinical diagnostics, intervention strategies, and resources, will greatly impact the team's comprehension of what will or will not work within the school setting.

The Level 2 conducted by the education member of the team typically starts with reviews of circumstantial information, file, and Level 1 protocol information as well as some preliminary interviews with the student or students of concern, administrators, school staff, and parents. The accumulated information is then discussed through further assessment and inquiry within the Level 2 investigation meeting along with the coordinated investigations of the investigative team's mental health specialist and law enforcement officer.

Student Interview

The following questions, adapted from the research and recommendations in chapter 3 (Mohandie, 2000; Johnson, 2000), serve as a guided interview if the student or students of concern are to be questioned as a part of the assessment (they may have already been interviewed by administration or law enforcement through the Level 1 assessment). (See appendix 2 C.) The questions move from a general discussion to details and facts, identifying protective factors and risk factors (Mohandie, 2000). The questions are only an outline and should be adapted or enhanced to address each unique situation.

1. Do you know why we are talking/why you are here?
2. Seems like there is something going on…what is it? What's your side of it?
3. How do you explain? (Watch for a shift of responsibility.)
4. Why are people (staff, student, parents) concerned? (Are there peer conflicts? What are the teacher/peer interaction dynamics? Is there an awareness of behavior? What is the affect?)

5. How is school? What's going on in school right now? (Are there conflicts, grudges, or events/motives justifying a violent act? What are successes within the school setting?)
6. How are things going outside of school...family, friends, community, work, and so on? (Are there aggravating circumstances?)
7. Who are your friends?
8. Who else is involved in this incident and how?
9. Who do you have to talk to and help you when you're in trouble? (Are there stabilizing factors, inhibitors, supports, and trusting relationships with adults?)
10. What kinds of things are you involved in...clubs, sports, church, scouts, and so on? (Are there activities that inhibit or discourage the violent action?)
11. Examining the facts and reports, it appears that _____ is being planned/considered. What is your part of the plan and who is in leadership (has control)?
12. Note student's state of mind/organization skills and potential for follow-through.
13. Other notes:

Educator's Level 2 Guided Investigation

In addition to educational, behavioral, and school issues, the investigative team's education member assesses situational factors increasing the risk of violence. The following items and questions are useful in composing a template guide for an educator's Level 2 threat assessment protocol. They are to be used, along with professional judgment, as an outline or guide for investigation. (For an example of an assessment protocol design, see appendix 2 D.)

Collect demographic information:
Account for name(s); age; grade; ID numbers; dates; school location; administrative case manager; risk level, type of aggression; status of case; follow-up date. (Avoid information that may be used as or perceived as profiling.)

Disclaimer:
Consider using a disclaimer such as "This protocol was developed as a structured outline to be used only by professionals trained in threat assessment, mental health/behavioral assessment, and psychoeducational assessment."

Note education and guardianship status:
Account for 504 status; special education; regular education status; adjudication; state/court wardship; foster care; special circumstances; disciplinary action.

Safety status:
Note current safety planning and supervision status.

Investigate situation or incident factors:

1. Describe concerns regarding threat(s).
2. Describe threat within the aggression continuum (see figure 4.1):
   ⇐ Mild / Moderate Aggression Extreme Aggression (Violence) ⇒
3. Describe any attack-related behavior in relevance to the above-noted threat (on aggression continuum):

   - Research, suspicious inquiry, information gathering, and so on
   - Rehearsal, simulation (repetitive viewing)
   - Acquisition of or attempt to acquire weapon and/or equipment
   - Arrangement of transportation
   - Ceremonial acts, final business
   - Scheduling, important date observance
   - Other
   - None (behavior not consistent with threat)

4. Are other students/people involved (supporting or allowing violent behavior, ideation, or planning)? Identify names, ages, and grades. Also note if a Level 1 or 2 assessment has been complete d on those who are involved.
5. What is the method of violence (physical, guns, sharps, bombs, other) and what is the availability of weaponry?
6. Are teachers, peers, or parents concerned with targeted or reactive aggressive behavior (is student seen as threatening, dangerous, or with apprehension)?
7. What is the main communication regarding the threat and the details of the threat (communication or "leakage" such as drawings, writings, music, journal, storytelling, bravado or bragging, verbal statements, predictions, Internet usage, texts, emails, behavioral gestures, other)? Were the communications made directly to potential target or to others regarding a target? Veiled, vague, or indirect? Specific or detailed? Simple or complex? Organized or disorganized? Suggesting an ultimatum? Indicating a fixed, ongoing theme?
8. What is the source of information regarding threat or behavior (rumor; first source information [leakage as noted above]; peer report; parent report; teacher, staff, or other adult report)?
9. What is the suspected intention of the threat (expressive or instrumental)?

10. What is the suspected motive that justifies a violent act or establishes control (injustice, rage, lost love, rejection, victimization, self-defense, recent loss, status change, humiliation, grievance, grudges, power, intimidation and bravado, extortion, other)?

11. Is there a plan for harm or lethal action and if so, does the plan:

   • Have detail or is it generalized or unclear?
   • Have a noted violent theme or is it a vague/veiled reference to threat?
   • Have an organized method or is it disorganized?
   • Have a simple or complex structure?
   • Have subjective plausibility?
   • Have objective plausibility?

12. Is suicidal ideation a feature of the threat or plan (Has a suicide assessment been completed?). Is there a history of suicidal ideation, gestures, and plans? If suicidal ideation is not directly indicated, is there a desire to be killed or a desire to die?

13. Is there a history of self-harm or self-mutilation?

14. JACA (de Becker, 1998):

   • Is there a justification to commit violence (blame, self-defense, etc.)?
   • Is there a perception that there are no alternatives to violence?
   • Are the consequences of a violent act viewed as acceptable?
   • Is there an ability to carry out a planned or methodical act?
   • Is there a perception of ability to carry out the act?

15. Are situations perceived as hopeless or desperate? Does the situation suggest:

   • An overwhelming stress?
   • Severe bullying, ridicule, or rejection?
   • Significant personal loss; loss of romantic or personal relationship?
   • Personal failure; discipline?
   • Jealousy?
   • Developmental health issue, psychosis, or thought disorder?

16. Are there indications of an existing or upcoming precipitating event (catalyst/final straw; anything that causes loss of face)?

17. Is there an excessive interest, orientation, and/or immersion in violence indicated by:

- Entertainment preferences (fantasy games, role-play games, readings, video or computer games, film, music, other entertainment)?
- Entertainment themes (sequential and specific to targeted or vendetta violence)?
- Role models and interests (notorious criminals; previous acts of violence; fictitious antisocial characters; weaponry; gangs)?
- Copycat implications?
- Entertainment that is used as a rehearsal or simulation for a violent act rather than amusement, entertainment, or shock?

18. What are the agitators and triggers?
19. Is violence viewed as necessary and imperative (see JACA elements above)?
20. What are inhibitors and protective factors (relationship with positive adult; family support; social support; positive attitude; prosocial involvement; prosocial beliefs or values; commitment to school; sports clubs; faith/church; pets; others)?
21. If targeted aggression, what is the intensity of:

- Ideation?
- Ongoing consideration of targeted act?
- Perseveration or notable focus on idea of violent act?
- Attack-related behavior (see list noted above)?
- Direct action toward attack?

22. Are there indications that the student(s) in this situation poses a threat to an identifiable target?
23. Is there target fixation and/or focus? Is attack scheduled?
24. What are target and guardian notification needs?

Conclude the situation factors by noting the level of concern:

- Unremarkable or low
- Decreasing
- Ongoing
- Escalating

Investigate school factors:

1. Academics
2. Attendance

3. Attachment to school
4. Behavioral history
5. Discipline history
6. Educational goals or plan
7. Other school concerns

Conclude the school factors by noting the level of concern:

- Unremarkable or low
- Decreasing
- Ongoing
- Escalating

Investigate social factors:

1. Are there healthy relationships with nonfamily adults (teachers, community leaders, neighborhood friends, church member, club members, etc.)?
2. Is there a history of victimization at school, home, and community (either real or perceived)?
3. What is the social status (high or accepted within mainstream and other groups; moderately accepted within mainstream; connected within small subculture or clique; disconnected/disinterested socially or self-committed loner with parallel social movement; rejected by mainstream and most subculture but maintains parallel social movement; rejected and marginalized but accepted within marginalized clique; completely rejected and marginalized; other)?
4. What is the peer group, if associated (culture, subculture, clique or marginalized clique, none, other?)
5. What is role within peer group, if associated (leadership; shared leadership; connected but reserved and varies in commitment to follow; is both leader and follower; follower; superficial, on the group's periphery or disconnected; toady, sycophant, or servant; other)?
6. Does peer group endorse antisocial thinking or dare risky behaviors?
7. Does peer group, culture, or community view aggression as an acceptable solution?
8. What is the community support level?

Conclude the social factors by noting the level of concern:

- Unremarkable or low
- Decreasing

- Ongoing
- Escalating

Investigate personal factors:

1. Have there been any recent changes in behavior and beliefs?
2. What are known behavioral patterns?
3. What are management skills for typical social conflict (prosocial, healthy range of response within developmental expectations; limited skills but responsive to help and suggestion; few skills and mostly avoidant; uses denial or argument; verbally combative; uses bravado and intimidation; physically combative; threats of aggression; other)?
4. What are strategies used to stop victimization, teasing, or rejection (avoids or reports trouble; appropriate use of assertiveness, negotiation, and adult resources; passively allows or compromises; enlists help of peers; bravado and posturing; threats or plans of revenge; physically fights back; full revenge; other)?
5. Is aggression personally viewed as an acceptable solution?
6. What are emotional coping reserves (healthy and developmentally appropriate; varies by mood and swing; immature for age; limited and shallow— few healthy strategies/emotional reserves are low; poorly developed strategies but accepts help; post-trauma or emotional distress interferes with use of skills/depletes skills quickly/has blocked skill development; other)?
7. What are anger management skills (within developmental expectations; limited but defuses quickly and accepts help and supervision; explosive and hostile; loses ability to reason and is unapproachable; loses control and is disruptive; other)?
8. Coping skills for change (flexible; optimistic; anticipates consequences; disinterested; passive; rigid; hypersensitive and irritable; intolerant; highly frustrated; other)?
9. Attitude (self as superior; injustice collector; sees self as an undeserved victim due to other's actions; entitled; delinquent; narcissistic; has healthy view of personal strengths and weaknesses; sees self as a failure; sees self as inferior, broken, or weak; sees self as an ongoing and deserving victim due to weaknesses; other)?
10. What is stress level (real or perceived)?
11. Are there indications of desperation or despair?
12. Is there an exaggerated need for attention, recognition, or notoriety?
13. What is compliance history (response to rules, authority, and structure)?
14. What are personal concerns regarding the situation (awareness of dysfunctional or troubled situation and wants to change; has awareness but

lacks concern or doesn't care; is unaware of dysfunctional or troubled situation)?
15. What is the level of trust with adults?
16. Address the following features of socialization and adjustment:

   • Exaggerated entitlement
   • Externalized blame
   • Superiority
   • Alienation
   • Dehumanizing behavior or attitude
   • Self-esteem
   • Empathy
   • Remorse
   • Manipulative and controlling, even at expense of others' physical comfort
   • Lacks moral beliefs (or values are maladjusted socially)

17. Has there been any recent loss or loss of status?
18. Is there a history of animal abuse?
19. Is there a history of fire-play?
20. Is there a history of property destruction?
21. Are there any signs or symptoms of depression (atypically indicated; sullen, moody, or apathetic)?
22. Is there a history of drug/alcohol use?
23. Are there any known mental health diagnoses?
24. Are there medications issues?
25. Is there a history of central nervous system damage or traumatic brain injury?
26. Is there a history of impulse or inattention problems?
27. Is there a history of emotional trauma?
28. Are there indications of victimization through abuse?
29. Has there been any previous psychiatric treatment or hospitalization?
30. If a history of treatment, what was response (amenable, guarded, poor response, resistive, hostile)?
31. Are there indications of positive future planning or vision?
32. Has there been any early police contact (prior to age twelve) or prior arrests or convictions (was offense aggressive)?
33. Is there a history of a willingness to hurt others?
34. Has there been a use of a weapon in past (to hurt other human beings)? Conclude the personal factors by noting the status of concern:

   • Unremarkable or low
   • Decreasing

- Ongoing
- Escalating

Investigate family dynamics factors:

1. Where is residence? Are there custody issues?
2. Siblings?
3. Is there a family history of domestic violence, mental illness, abuse, substance abuse, criminal activity, arrests and/or incarceration (for aggressive or violent crime)?
4. What is the level of support from the parent/guardian?
5. What are family dynamics and relationships (parental, sibling)?
6. Do parents and/or family view criminal behavior or criminal violence as acceptable?
7. Is there a lack of supervision within the household?
8. Do parents/guardians have control of household? What are limits on behavior?
9. Is there computer access within the home? Is there unsupervised computer access?
10. What is extended-family support level?

Conclude the family dynamic factors by noting the level of concern:

- Unremarkable or low
- Decreasing
- Ongoing
- Escalating

Investigate gang involvement factors:

1. Identification:
2. What is level of involvement?
3. What is role in gang (leader, instigator, follower, toady)?
4. Is there an expressed commitment?
5. Is there a willingness to act antisocially on behalf of gang?
6. Are there records of delinquent or aggressive gang acts to date?
7. Is there a gang-oriented motive, target, or plan?
8. Are there communications suggesting gang-related attack?
9. Is behavior consistent with communication?
10. Is there attack-related behavior associated with gang goals or motive?
11. Are there means and weaponry available to carry out attack?

12. Is the action targeted aggression?
13. What are agitators?
14. Are there any inhibiting factors?

Conclude the gang involvement factors by noting the level of concern:

- Unremarkable or low
- Decreasing
- Ongoing
- Escalating

Note other concerns and information:

1. Other concerns:
2. Collateral information:
3. Context of aggression:
   - Reaction/affectation:
     Expressive
     Stress relief
     Bravado and intimidation
     Power, resistance, or revenge
     Attention seeking
     Other
   - Targeted and premeditated:
     Rampage and theatrical expression
     Stealth and discretion
     Relational
     Other
   - Instrumental purpose:
     Control, intimidation, or extortion
     Vendetta, grievance, grudge, revenge
     Other
   - Gang
   - Influenced by drugs and alcohol

Determine type of aggression and level of risk:

The most important feature of a Level 2 threat assessment is the use of supervision and intervention strategies to decrease risk; however, there is often a question regarding the "level" of risk indicated through the assessment.

The following is a rubric used to compartmentalize risk factors and thus assign a level of concern. It is not a quantifiable measure nor is it meant to be a label. It is designed to further guide the process of improving safety through prudent and appropriate planning (see appendix 2 E). The rubric is divided into sections, one for targeted aggression and one for reactive aggression. Each section is divided into a behavioral definition and a risk definition.

TARGETED AGGRESSION: The attacker considers and selects a particular target prior to attack. The consideration occurs through the process of an idea with motive, planning, preparation, location, and eventually scheduling.

- Low or Minor Risk

  o Vague or indirect information contained within the threat is inconsistent.
  o Threat is implausible or lacks detail; lacks realism.
  o Context of threat suggests that action is unlikely.
  o Little history of serious risk factors or dangerous behavior.
  o Inhibitors are present.
  o Behavior that is aggressive but has little potential for physical injury. Minor bullying.
  o Threats are for stress relief, bravado, and affect.

- Moderate Risk

  o Indication of some premeditation or planning with general implications of place, time, target (still short of detailed plan).
  o No strong indication of preparatory steps, although there may be some veiled reference or ambiguous evidence of threat possibility (reference to gun availability, movie with theme, or sequence-specific violent act).
  o Some inhibitors present as well as an indication of desire for help.
  o Targeted threat or behavior is aggression that has intention for physical injury (but not serious or lethal injury).

- High Risk

  o Threat or behavior is targeted and appears to pose serious danger to others.
  o Threat is direct, specific, detailed, and plausible.
  o Information suggests the presence of concrete preparations, target, and planning.
  o Few inhibitors present.
  o Sees no or few alternatives to action.
  o Identified precipitating events with justification and the acceptance of consequences.
  o Likely to qualify for immediate arrest or hospitalization.

- Imminent Risk

    o Same criteria as "High Risk for Harm" but with the possession of weapons and a situation that is scheduled or clearly close to dangerous or explosive.

REACTIVE/AFFECTIVE AGGRESSION: The attacker acts in an emotional or highly aroused state in response to a perceived challenge, threat, insult, or other affront. It is often a temporary, explosive, or impulsive act without premeditation, planning, plotting, or specific targeting. Reactive behavior can be a function within a pattern of socialization as some attackers search for excuses or opportunities to be angry and aggressive, without any predetermined target.

- Low or Minor Risk

    o Responsive to interventions.
    o Has little or no history of affective hostility or aggressive reaction.
    o Behavior is reactively aggressive and has little potential for physical injury.
    o Behavior is for stress relief, bravado, and affect.

- Moderate Risk

    o Interventions are effective but student can be resistive and hostile given the identified agitation. Somewhat unstable and requires extra staff effort to restrain.
    o Peers and staff are frequently on guard.
    o Aggressive behavior may cause physical injury but is not intended to be serious or lethal.

- High Risk

    o Behavior is frequently impulsive and reactively aggressive.
    o Intention or outcome is close to serious injury or is serious injury with the possibility of lethal injury. Interventions are frequent and considerable in order to restrain aggression.
    o Student is unresponsive or has limited response to intervention.

Determine supervision strategies and interventions:

The Level 2 investigative team completes the assessment by consulting with the Level 1 site team on interventions and supervision strategies. It is helpful to have a list or template of resources and intervention options available to the schools and community (see appendix 2 F). Such a template serves the investigative team as well as the full student threat assessment team.

Prior to providing the recommendations to the Level 1 site team, the education member of the investigative team should make the following disclaimer: "These recommendations were generated through the efforts of the student threat assessment team (STAT) and are for consideration in the management of threatening or dangerous circumstances involving students. STAT is a consultation team that assesses risk of violence and assists case managers with the application of resources to manage and decrease the possibility of attack, protect potential targets, and support students to develop and employ healthy and safe coping strategies."

The following are some examples of recommendations available within the Salem, Oregon, community. Other districts may differ in available resources, but the general idea is to list out useful strategies and interventions that will decrease the risk of aggression.

1. First Steps:

   - Staff case through Mid-Valley Student Threat Assessment Team (STAT) on (date): _____.
   - Administrator will request further assessment if risk circumstances escalate. Call: (coordinator of STAT).
   - Continue with Level 1 student supervision plan.
   - Notify and warn potential victims. (Parent/guardian of targeted student notified.)

2. Student Options:

   - Individual accountability plan: No-harm contract/Student will self-manage.
   - Initiate suicide assessment. (Use district suicide protocol.)
   - Student will identify triggers, agitators, and agree to "safe room" or resource of support.
   - Diversion.

3. School Options:

   - Protective response initiated by security department.
   - Alert staff and teachers on need-to-know basis.
   - Review educational plan.
   - Specialized class/alternative class or track.
   - Travel card and time accountability.
   - Late arrival/early dismissal.
   - Modification of day or schedule.
   - Entry/exit check with_____.

- Social skill–building program.
- Increase supervision in following settings: _____.
- Decrease or eliminate pass time or unsupervised time.
- Frequent/random search of backpack/purse, locker, pockets, and so on by school personnel.
- Assign identified staff to build trusting relationship through check-in or mentorship:

  o Administrator
  o Mentor
  o CDS/counselor
  o School resource officer
  o Teacher
  o Other

- Provide means by which student may safely report and discuss thoughts or intentions to harm others and receive appropriate intervention.
- Identify and further develop activities, relationships, or things of value that inhibit possibility of acting out.
- Other interventions or supervision strategies that will directly address the triggers and agitators identified through assessment.
- Child development specialist/school counselor intervention:
- Refer to prevention and intervention resource specialist or other school resource.
- Consider placement change (administrative transfer, interim alternative educational setting (IAES), expulsion, etc., per district policy. (District may unilaterally remove student to IAES, but IEP team decides actual placement if student is receiving specialized instruction. See below.)
- Refer to school special education or 504 team to consider referral for evaluation.
- If student has IEP or 504 plan, refer to special education team or 504 team to consider:

  o Further evaluation
  o Reviewing goals and placement options
  o Referral to alternative educational placement
  o Increasing supervision in the following setting:_____.
  o Home supervision (with access to education) pending further assessment, adaptations, or action

- Continue to monitor communications and behavior for an escalation of risk.
- Safety planning at site of attendance (home school; SPED (Special Education) placement; alternative education; in-district transfer).

4. Family/Home Options:

- Strategize safety options/planning.
- Parents contacted and will provide the following supervision/intervention:_____.
- Safety-proof home.
- Referral for domestic violence intervention and safety planning.
- Parent training classes.

5. Community Options:

- Referral to community youth service team (YST).
- Refer for STAT mental health evaluation.
- Refer to anger management program.
- Refer to mentoring programs.
- Notify probation/parole officer.
- Explore faith community programs as identified by parents/guardians.
- Foster positive community activities, interests.
- Explore grant money assistance for inhibitors or other prosocial activities of interest.
- Refer to Juvenile Department family support program.
- Referral to substance abuse intervention.
- Review mental health evaluation options.
- Review of counseling or therapy options.
- Juvenile Department supervision and release/safety plan.

MENTAL HEALTH

The mental health member of the investigation team also completes a threat assessment protocol, tailored to the perspective of the public mental health practitioner.

Community mental health participates in both the investigative team and the full STAT consultation staffing. As a member of the investigative team, the mental health professional or MHP's role includes analyzing the communicated threat and behavior of the identified student. As opposed to traditional mental health roles of determining diagnosis for the purpose of treatment, the mental health professional "articulates behavioral patterns, translates behavior in the context of assessing violence potential, and develops strategies to manage and contain potentially violent behavior instead of authoring treatment plans" (Gelles et al., 2002).

From this perspective the MHP assists the team in developing a management strategy that focuses on the safety of the victim as well as the safety

of the perpetrator. This is a consultative role to school administration and
law enforcement, which remain responsible for case management. The MHP
perspective and ongoing consultation offered to the school brings out the
strength of the investigative partnership, providing a broader and more comprehensive assessment of the identified threat.

According to Gelles et al. (2002), the MHP's role "is to support the investigation by acting as a translator of behavior and communication. It is important that the mental health professional maintains their consultative role and
not become actively engaged in the investigation." In this consultative role,
the MHP should have:

- Knowledge of community resources regarding mental health and youth
  services
- Understanding of clinical diagnosis, mental health issues, and an ability to
  translate technical psychiatric language to members of the team
- Mental health evaluation skills and an understanding of the evaluation options within the community
- The ability to provide in-depth mental health assessments from a threat
  assessment perspective when requested
- A functional awareness and understanding of local mental health systems
  and access options such as immediate hospitalization, counseling services,
  indigent services, crisis assessment options, long-term hospitalization, re-
  spite, and in-school resources
- A process perspective and an appreciation of the unique perspectives of
  those within the education system and law enforcement

Threat assessment is different from mental health counseling or the traditional mental health evaluation. In counseling, the goal is to assist the client,
through empathy and the guidance process, to "feel better" and improve life.
Using a diagnostic process, mental health evaluation examines a client's
mental and emotional hygiene for the indication of treatment needs. Both of
these approaches can be too narrow to serve the threat assessment process.

Threat assessment examines the unique circumstantial and environmental issues by assessing the situation, including mental health issues,
for risk factors and the indicated management and intervention needs
that immediately address that risk. Limiting an MHP to only a mental
health evaluation or an assessment to determine counseling needs would
decrease the mental health contribution. Furthermore, limiting the MHP
may also decrease the effectiveness of the overall threat assessment by ignoring the unique dynamic of mental health and the situational variables,
most important to the process.

With that in mind, the actual investigation process for the mental health professional uses an empirically guided evaluation. Empirically guided evaluation, sometimes referred to as structured clinical assessment, uses instruments or checklists to help structure or guide the collection and analysis of appropriate information. This may involve an assessment of a situation with one or more individuals at risk, so each individual is viewed through a mental health assessment lens that is informed by the base rates for violence within the individual's population, and by relevant risk factors known to be related to the risk of violent behavior.

Risk judgments based on guided or structured assessments have been shown to produce greater rates of accuracy than those based on unstructured assessments or traditional mental health evaluations. This said, standard psychological tests and other instruments traditionally used in guided professional judgment are of questionable utility to school-based, targeted violence risk assessments. The best approach is to use an empirically guided assessment tool combined with the careful observation of the risk factors identified in the earlier chapters. Such an approach requires training in threat assessment and collaborative decision making.

Mental Health Professional's Guided Level 2 Investigation

The following are two recommendations (but not a complete list of options) for assessment tools that can be used to guide the mental health portion of a threat assessment.

Manual for the Structured Assessment of Violence Risk in Youth (SAVRY) by Randy Borum, Patrick Bartel, and Adelle Forth, University of South Florida, 2002. This instrument is based on structured professional judgment model. It is composed of twenty-four risk items divided into three sections: historical, social/contextual, and individual and protective factors.

An adaptation of Eric Johnson's questionnaire from *Advanced Topics in the Assessment of Youth Violence* (Johnson, 2000). This instrument is composed of nine sections: individual risk factors; family risk factors; peer/community risk factors; school risk factors; alcohol/drug risk factors; mental health risk factors; delinquency risk factors; weapons risk factors; inventory of aggressive/violent behavior.

The following questions are adapted from Eric Johnson's inventories and are a good template for guiding the mental health assessment (see appendix 2 G) during the Level 2 investigation:

* Individual Risk Factors (escalating, deescalating, or stable)

    o Early behavior problems (before age ten)

o Risk taking
o Problems managing aggression

- Family Risk Factors (escalating, deescalating, or stable)

  o Severe marital/family strife
  o Family aggression in community
  o Antisocial parents
  o Poor parenting practices (lax/punitive)
  o Child maltreatment (neglect and physical abuse)
  o Domestic violence
  o Family endorses violence
  o Sibling delinquency
  o Early parent-child separations
  o Poverty

- Peer/Community Risk Factors (escalating, deescalating, or stable)

  o Poor peer relations (unpopular, delinquent peers)
  o Availability of firearms
  o Peers/adults endorse violence

- School Risk Factors (escalating, deescalating, or stable)

  o Frequent disciplinary problems
  o Truancy/skipping school
  o Low commitment to school
  o Poor grades

- Alcohol/Drug Risk Factors (escalating, deescalating, or stable)
- Early alcohol/drug use (six to eleven years)
- Serious substance use
- Sells drugs
- Mental Health Risk Factors (escalating, deescalating, or stable)
- Hyperactive/impulsive/inattention
- Delinquency Risk Factors (escalating, deescalating, or stable)
- Early police contacts (six to eleven years)
- Prior arrests/convictions
- Gang membership (current/past/wannabe)
- Aggressive/violent offense(s)
- Weapons Risk Factors (escalating, deescalating, or stable)

  o Has used weapons to harm others
  o Has attempted to procure weapons

- Inventory of Aggressive/Violent Behavior (escalating, deescalating, or stable)
  - o Unusual interest in violence
  - o Aggression causing serious injury
  - o Frequent acts of aggression

As noted above, in addition to the work on the investigatory team, the MHP may conduct a mental health evaluation that further examines the impact of mental health issues on increased risk of violence.

This evaluation is done through interviews with student and family. The purpose of using this option is the further examination of a student's mental health condition and further insight into the student's motivation in making the threat or behaving in a threatening manner.

This is especially beneficial where there are either clear mental health issues or to correct the often-misguided public perception that only "crazy people" make threats. (It is only in a very small number of cases where symptoms of psychosis are present and directed toward the victim.) The evaluation can also determine whether hospitalization or other mental health interventions are needed.

Since most mental health professionals lack the training needed to conduct mental health evaluations or assessments of students who make threats of violence, it is important that the MHP doing the work pursue the appropriate training. Furthermore, the threat assessment team MHP should have experience in behavioral assessment, knowledge of violence risk assessment literature, experience in working with law enforcement investigation, and experience in crisis interview and intervention.

LAW ENFORCEMENT

Law enforcement plays an integral part in any threat assessment and threat management program. The Safe School Initiative (Vossekuil et al., 2002), conducted by the United States Secret Service and the United States Department of Education, has identified law enforcement as a primary participant in school threat assessment systems. Programs that are in existence today give support and verification to this recommendation.

Threat assessment requires the collection of facts and the investigation of information suggesting the potential for violence. Law enforcement personnel are trained to conduct these investigations and have the tools available to gather information that is not available to the other disciplines that a threat assessment team comprises. Law enforcement can gather critical information through computerized criminal histories on all involved parties and check records to determine the history and nature of past police contacts, firearms purchase information, and out-of-area criminal information.

Law enforcement personnel have the training and natural inquisitive nature to conduct thorough and in-depth investigations. They use the investigative process and knowledge to obtain necessary facts in a given case and can further the perspective of any assessment through their street knowledge and instincts. Law enforcement officers also have the resources to obtain peripheral information, not only on the subjects of the assessments but also on others who may have considerable impact and knowledge of the subject. This is essential, as friends, relatives, and associates often have a part in the threatening situation, either directly or indirectly.

Law enforcement also has the ability to efficiently obtain information and/ or intelligence through resources such as narcotics enforcement teams, street crimes teams, and patrol resources. They have the ability to utilize such resources to conduct "knock and talk" investigations, surveillance, crime analysis, and field interviews as a means of learning about the dynamics of a situation involving one or more people of concern.

Law enforcement has a unique familiarity with the criminal justice system and an understanding of court, prosecution, and custody procedures. Furthermore, law enforcement has the needed credibility within those systems to obtain cooperation and results. Since the professionals within the courts, prosecution, corrections, and the majority of law enforcement have only a limited knowledge of threat assessment, it is important for law enforcement officers who are trained in threat assessment and management to effectively communicate and inform the rest of the legal system.

Through appropriate, timely, and tactful information sharing, law enforcement can incorporate the threat assessment process into the court system. Furthermore, by articulating the process of threat assessment and management, writing accurate reports, testifying in court, and providing training to others, officers trained in threat assessment can secure partnerships and cooperation within the criminal justice system as well as other public agencies.

Law enforcement also has the legal authority to take immediate enforcement action when necessary and make custody arrests based on probable cause. While this is not always necessary, it is sometimes vital in order to secure a situation and prevent an act of violence. Officers have the training, the tools, the resources, and the system in place to take this immediate action when safety becomes an issue.

Finally, law enforcement has the authority to conduct searches and seizures and obtain search warrants based on probable cause. Without this ability to seize evidence, weapons, and obtain information, a threat assessment team would be severely hampered in its ability to assess and manage threats within a community.

The following is a list of the law enforcement officer's duties during a Level 1 assessment or a Level 2 threat assessment:

- Safety of all persons.
- Investigate and interview if necessary for crimes committed and take appropriate action.
- Provide appropriate background information on suspects and also victims (juvenile record, family history, personal contacts, gang information).
- Be a sounding board for the process. Use skills in investigations to help others from jumping to conclusions. Maintain a "facts"-oriented investigation.
- Instruct staff on how to gather facts (who, what, when, where, why, and how).
- Inform staff of existing laws regarding their duties in responding to threats.
- Maintain the team awareness of state laws regarding juveniles. (In Oregon, for example, ORS.166.370 regarding the possession of firearm or dangerous weapon.)

Law Enforcement Member's Guided Level 2 Investigation

The following questions provide a template for guiding the law enforcement assessment during the Level 2 investigation (see appendix 2 H):

1. What are the names and ages of siblings?
2. Is child protective services and welfare involved? If so, what is the name of the caseworker?
3. Is a juvenile probation officer involved? If so, what is the officer's name?
4. Describe the threat, dangerous situation, or aggressive action.
5. Were the threats direct or indirect, detailed, or vague?
6. Does the student have a plan to hurt others? If yes, is the plan plausible or implausible?
7. Does the student have an identified target or targets? If so, describe the relationship with the target or suspected target.
8. Does the student have access to firearms?
9. Are firearms and/or bombs a significant part of the student's persona?
10. What is the status of the JACA elements? (de Becker, 1998)

   - Justification
   - Alternatives
   - Consequences
   - Ability

11. Are students or staff afraid of the student?
12. Does the student use drugs or alcohol? If yes, what is the student using or suspected of using? How often is the student using?
13. Does the student have a history of police contact?

14. Does the student have a history of juvenile justice involvement?
15. Does the student have a past history of misconduct at school, including suspensions or expulsions?
16. Does the student have a past history of bringing prohibited items on campus?
17. Does the student have a history of animal abuse or fire-play?
18. Does the student have irrational beliefs and ideas, including unreciprocated romantic obsession? Has the student's behavior escalated in severity or frequency during the last six months?
19. What is student's social status?
20. Does the student have positive activities or interests that would inhibit them from acting out in a violent manner?
21. Has the student expressed thoughts of suicide?
22. Does the student suffer from known mental health issues?
23. Has the student been victimized by their peers in the past eighteen months?
24. What is the reaction of the student's parents or caregivers to the situation?
25. Does the student's family, including siblings, have a history of gang or criminal justice involvement?
26. Does the student have a parent who has been convicted or incarcerated for a violent crime?
27. Is there a family member currently in the armed forces?
28. Is there a history of domestic violence in the student's family? If yes, does the student identify with their mother or father?
29. Have the student's previous schools been contacted?

Law enforcement officers preparing to conduct threat assessments through the Level 2 process should pursue further training and readings suggested by this manual's bibliography and website or contact one of the authors for recommendations.

OTHER AGENCY INVOLVEMENT

In addition to education, law enforcement, and public mental health, there are other youth-serving agencies that assist and consult on the student threat assessment team. The state youth authority (OYA in Oregon) and the county juvenile justice department both sit on the team and offer their perspectives on risk, management, and resources. Furthermore, with adjudicated youth, both agencies can offer considerable assistance with planning, placement, and supervision options and facilitate the future involvement of the justice system.

Finally, the investigative team is the "point guard" of the student threat assessment team. Training and commitment are important to anyone doing the work but essential to the members doing the primary investigation. That training, along with the unique agency and professional perspectives of the team's investigators, provide the balance and efficiency needed to accurately assess situations of potential violence and make response recommendations that accurately address risk variables. Shared community responsibility and ownership begins with the investigative team and is then reinforced by the entire STAT collaboration.

Chapter Eight

Level 2 Student Threat Assessment Team Operations

John Van Dreal, Martin Speckmaier

The consultation staffing, conducted by the entire membership of STAT, occurs on a regular basis (weekly if possible) and addresses all new cases as well as the follow-up information of past cases. STAT functions as a consultation team and focuses on the assessment of situations that pose a threat to school district students and staff as well as assists with supervision planning strategies and resource exploration. STAT does not mandate interventions, predict the future, or possess the authority to bypass or override the policy or procedure of any agency or institution (this includes the IEP process for placement in special education).

Even through the Level 2 assessment process, the school site team (Level 1 team) maintains the authority and responsibility for final decisions about management, intervention, and supervision. Case management always remains with the site team at the attending school.

TEAM MEETINGS

As noted in chapter 6, when reviewing new cases, the team follows the following format:

1. *Up to 10 minutes:* Case manager (school administrator/counselor, agency caseworker, and/or police officer) reviews threat or incident, concerns, current supervision and intervention, and outcomes of current supervision and intervention.
2. *Up to 15 minutes:* STAT investigative team (Level 2) presents results of assessment. The education lead may provide a short summary of risk factors to assist the team members with needed information (see appendix 1).

3. *Up to 20 minutes:* STAT conducts further assessment, consults on supervision strategies, and explores community resources. (See appendix 2 J for
information glossaries to assist and facilitate the team.)

As the team conducts the consultation and further assessment, members
attempt to be sensitive to time limitations and follow the following structural
rules (Mohandie, 2000; Corcoran and Cawood, 2003; de Becker, 1998):

- Pay attention to intuition, but focus on facts.
- Focus on behavior, not profile traits.
- Review all factors as they exist within context.
- Examine behavioral progress, changes, and movement into the targeting
  continuum.
- Confirm information, confirm impressions.
- Address all investigative questions regarding risk.
- Focus on prevention and inhibitors, not prediction. (Counseling, support,
  confrontation, access restrictions and increased supervision, arrest, pros-
  ecution, etc., are all inhibitors. Use the inhibitor that best matches the risk.)
- Remember the goal...identify risk, decrease that risk, and improve the
  psychological safety and learning environment.
- Pursue long-term intervention only if time allows. Keep an eye on immediate risk factors and solving short-term management issues.

Since STAT relies upon its participating agencies' time and commitment,
a team that is well trained, invested in the work, and aware of the time
limitations is vital to the functioning and efficiency of the process. A healthy
process balances assessment with the exploration of resource options and
management.

CONFIDENTIALITY AND INFORMATION SHARING

Any district, agency, or collaboration of agencies considering the formation
of a threat assessment team should pursue legal counsel prior to its implementation. Of specific note are information-sharing policies. Most of education
information sharing is regulated by a federal law called FERPA or the Family
Education Rights and Privacy Act. The following is taken from the defini-
tions and explanations of FERPA (www.ed.gov/offices/fpco/ferparegs.html).

FERPA is a federal law that protects the privacy of education records or
any records that contain information directly relating to a student and that are
maintained by the educational institution, agency, or a person acting for the

agency or institution. FERPA permits disclosure of personally identifiable information without consent in certain circumstances, including:

- To school officials with legitimate educational interests as established by...criteria listed in the annual notification of rights under FERPA and published annually by individual schools or school districts.
- To appropriate officials in health and safety emergencies...so long as the information is necessary for the receiving party to deal with the emergency nature of the situation and...made to protect the health or safety of the student or others. This provision is limited to specific situations that present imminent danger to a student or other students, members of the school community...or to a situation that requires the immediate need for information from education records in order to avert or diffuse a serious threat to the safety or health of a student or other individuals.
- To comply with a lawfully issued judicial order or subpoena.

Information from education records may be shared with police, social services, or other community representatives who are serving on a school's established threat assessment committee, if they are school officials with legitimate educational interests in accordance with the school's established criteria. Such individuals may not use that information for any purpose other than consideration on that committee, nor may they take the information back to their agencies or share it with anyone else except under the provisions of FERPA. Education records are:

- Records that contain information directly related to a student and are maintained by an educational institution or third party.
- The records can be in various media forms.

But they are not:
- Directory information
- Sole possession records
- Law enforcement unit records (see below)
- Student hit lists
- Other general communications by students

The exceptions to FERPA are:
- To officials of another school, district, or postsecondary
- Upon court order or subpoena
- Release of information to appropriate authorities in a health and/or safety emergency

A school's law enforcement unit's records are excluded from the definition of "education records." If such records include information from a student's education records, that information may not be disclosed to outside agencies unless one of the exceptions to FERPA's consent provisions applies.

FERPA does not protect the confidentiality of information, in general. It protects information from education records. Therefore, if students or staff witness or hear of a student's behavior, communication, or ideas and then orally share that information with members of the threat assessment committee, the information is not protected by FERPA since it was not provided through an education record.

FERPA does not have a personal liability recourse. Claims are made through the U.S. Department of Education against schools. Personal claims are made through state law.

To summarize: FERPA should not be an impediment to a threat assessment system. FERPA governs only records, not observations, communications, and so on. And it does not permit a private right of action.

In 2009, FERPA was reconsidered and adapted. The new regulations impose a "rational basis" test on a school's decisions to disclose information in emergency situations. "The Department [of Education] will not substitute its judgment for that of the agency or institution if, based on the information available at the time...there is a rational basis for the agency's or institution's determination that a health or safety emergency exists."

Leroy Rooker, then director of the U.S. Department of Education's Family Policy Compliance Office, noted: "We wanted to strike that balance between privacy and safety and certainly emphasize that safety on a campus is paramount. As long as you can articulate what that emergency was, we're not going to be in the business of second-guessing you on that."

Still, according to the new rules, administrators must document what emergency circumstances prompted their decision to disclose information. If you can articulate in writing the nature of the emergency that prompted the release of information, the USDOE will not be second-guessing you. Totality of the situation is critical.

And finally, most state systems as well as the federal department of education (Fein et al., 2002) encourage information sharing where public safety is concerned. The following are Oregon laws and administrative rules that allow the sharing of information under health and safety situations, intervention prior to a youth's adjudication and during a youth's adjudication:

• ORS 336.187 A and B allow discussion and protective reporting. This applies to student threat assessment teams, especially with an MOU (memorandum of understanding, see appendix 2 K) stating confidentiality rules and procedures. Conversations can take place between education, law enforcement, and child protective agencies.

- ORS 339.312 suggests a safe-schools alliance between schools, the Juvenile Department, and law enforcement.
- OAR 581-021-0380 outlines health and safety emergencies that obligate discussion and reporting between education and other agencies.

The threat assessment system reviewed in this manual is a two-tier system with a site-based component and a community-based component composed of members from educational districts and institutions, law enforcement, public mental health, and other youth-serving public agencies.

The chapters in section 3, as well as the appendix, contain the protocols necessary for the implementation of this system. The protocols and forms are designed to be minimal in busywork and avoid bureaucratic interference and red tape. The system is designed as an implementation of the assessment recommendations from the experts throughout the nation as well as a means to examine information in an efficient and timely manner. To do so is paramount to successful assessment and management.

Chapter Nine

Organizing a Student Threat Assessment System

John Van Dreal

As with most community collaborations, the adult threat management team and student threat assessment team encountered a number of barriers to the development and establishment of a system. Both teams lacked resources, as well as available services; agencies experienced differences in philosophy and purpose; policies related to information sharing were absent or unclear; agencies lacked the appropriate training to do the assessment and management work.

The process used to overcome these and other hurdles, as well as the process for the development and implementation of a threat assessment system, can be a bit complicated but does not need to be overwhelming. To start, consider the following suggestions:

NEED, JUSTIFICATION, AND AUTHORIZATION

Determine if your district needs a threat assessment system and define the need in objective terms. Pursue administrative approval to explore the development of a system and authorization for the time and resources to begin the process. The process often requires the development of an infrastructure that defines a new system or may even change an existing system. The process often begins with the implementation of a strategic planning process followed by a proposed schedule for development and implementation.

Strong leadership is essential and should be done by a "champion" or "boundary spanner" (Fein et al., 2002), someone who is deeply committed to the project, respected within his or her agency, related with community partners, knowledgeable about the community, understanding and respectful of the different dynamics within the community's youth-serving agencies, and comfortable moving through and within those agencies.

99

COMMUNITY OWNERSHIP,
COMMITMENT, AND RESPONSIBILITY

The foundation of STAT is a community collaboration of key, youth-serving agencies committed to school and community safety. It is an inter-dependent collaborative group characterized by high trust levels, efficient communication systems, and group decision making with equal input from all partners.

Accomplishing such collaboration requires building a coalition of partnerships focused on achieving fundamental changes in the way agencies share information, resources, student referrals, and responsibility for public safety. To follow the recommendations of the Safe School Initiative, membership must include education, public mental health, and law enforcement.

Beyond that, consider juvenile justice, the state youth authority, the district attorney's office, the courts, child protective services, and other youth-serving community agencies. Also seek input from other professionals in the community who work with an at-risk population or encounter threatening and dangerous behavior as a feature of their work (crisis workers, domestic violence interventionists, etc.).

The representatives selected should be knowledgeable about their own agencies' policies, practices, and funding structures. The partners should consider their commitment to the development of a functional student threat assessment team as one that supersedes their individual interests as isolated agents.

Each representative should have the decision-making authority necessary to conceptualize and approve changes in practice required by the new team protocol. Team members participate with equal status, as consultants with valued opinions; thus, rank or title are not features of standing or authority within the collaboration. Such relationship dynamics assist the team to create a shared vision for ongoing partnership and success within the task of threat assessment and management.

The following recommendations are an adaptation from the list of member attributes suggested by the Safe School Initiative (Fein et al., 2002):

- An ability to relate well to others (staff, colleagues, other professionals, students, parents, and public)
- An awareness and sensitivity to the difference between harming and helping in an intervention
- A reputation for fairness and trustworthiness (throughout the community of agencies that serve youth)
- A questioning, analytical, and even skeptical mindset

- Training in the collection and evaluation of information from multiple sources; an ability to "investigate"
- Discretion and an appreciation for the importance of keeping information confidential and an understanding of the possible harm that may result with an inappropriate release of information
- Familiarity with the current issues of school and community safety
- The ability to serve as a formal link or liaison between various systems and meet regularly within those systems (a "boundary spanner" who believes in the project and the process)
- In-depth knowledge about their own organization, resource availability, and both political and ethical boundaries; someone who can speak to the agency's commitment and decision process as well as their contribution
- Credibility, respect, and strong interpersonal skills; supported by their agency's administration

ESTABLISH THE POLICY AND PROCEDURES NECESSARY FOR FUNCTIONING

Consult legal counsel. If needed, shop for examples. Approach districts with established threat assessment systems and request copies of their policies and procedures. Salem-Keizer Public Schools and other members of the Mid-Valley Threat Assessment Team have assisted many districts as they navigated their way through the development and implementation process. Know FERPA as well as your local and state laws that pertain to multiagency collaborations, confidentiality, and information sharing within a threat assessment and management context.

ORGANIZE RESOURCES, DESIGN SYSTEM, AND REFINE

Use this manual and the material noted in the References, Additional Readings, and Resources of this book to identify resources and systems recommendations. Examine the model in this manual, as well as other existing models, for strengths that will enhance your system. Carefully examine and measure your resources and limitations and consider as many in-kind efforts as possible to hold costs down. Then scrutinize and refine. Choose your timeline to allow for the process of multiagency approval, attorney consultation, and the obtaining of memorandums of understanding (see appendix 2 K).

TRAIN LEVEL 2 AND LEVEL 1 TEAMS

First train your Level 2 multiagency team. Once you have your lead educator, train your Level 1 site teams. Then fully implement and refine.

MAINTENANCE OF PROGRAM, TROUBLESHOOTING, AND ONGOING TRAINING

Identify weaknesses in your new system and gaps in services; utilize existing resources and mechanisms to compensate. Use your collaborative efforts and connections to build greater resources. As your team builds in skill and experience, evaluate and maximize communications.

Considering these recommendations will aid a team as they prepare for the challenges of systems change and collaboration building. The writers of this manual are also available for consultation with communities and school districts that are considering the development of a threat assessment system.

Section IV

Further Applications

Chapter Ten

Other Security and Behavioral Issues on School Campuses

Rod Swinehart, Ray Byrd, John Van Dreal, Shelley Spady

The majority of this book is devoted to addressing student aggression, an ongoing and important issue. However, other safety issues can impede the development of a school's healthy milieu. This chapter addresses those issues and provides recommendations for further action. Specifically, the material attends to physical site security, personal security, suicide assessment, firesetter assessment, and sexual incident management.

SITE SECURITY

The campus's physical security can be well addressed through a system titled crime prevention through environmental design or CPTED. Most law enforcement departments have staff trained in CPTED and can be of considerable assistance in providing recommendations for improving a physical location's security.

The physical appearance of a building has a great deal to do with crime prevention. James Q. Wilson and George Kelling developed the "broken windows" thesis (Kelling, 1982) to explain the signaling function of neighborhood characteristics. This thesis suggests that the following sequence of events can be expected in a deteriorating neighborhood. First, the evidence of decay (accumulated trash, broken windows, deteriorated building exteriors) remains in the neighborhood for a long period of time.

As a result, people who live and work in the area feel more vulnerable and begin to withdraw. They become less willing to intervene in neighborhood problems or to maintain public order (for example, to attempt to break up individuals or groups loitering on street corners).

They also are less willing to address physical signs of deterioration. Sensing this, possible offenders become bolder and intensify their harassment and vandalism. Residents become yet more fearful and withdraw further from community involvement and upkeep. The atmosphere then attracts offenders from outside the area, who sense that it has become a vulnerable and thus amenable site for crime.

The following are a few highlights from CPTED that address the "broken windows" pattern of decline and that can be adapted to a school site.

Exterior

Construct the exterior and grounds of a location to allow the observation of anyone approaching. Start from the roadway approach to the building. Locate the visitor parking lot where it can be viewed from the office. Fencing and/ or landscaping should define the borders of the property. Even a short fence with observable gates located at the front of the property can be an adequate deterrent because it requires that people use a controlled access. If a person wants to approach unseen, they must either search for an opening or climb over the fence. And such suspicious behavior will increase the likelihood that staff, neighbors, or the general public will notice and report.

Landscaping should be low and well groomed to prevent opportunities for concealment. Landscaping should also define walking paths. (A person outside the defined walking path will attract attention.) Posted signage should direct visitors to the main entrance to "check in." Signage should also warn that visitors "may be subject to video surveillance," which is also a deterrent. All signs should be highly visible and well maintained.

With exception to the main entrance, all exterior doors should be locked. This forces the visitor to enter the main entrance, where they will be observed and where their movement can be controlled. (Entry through any other door will re-quire increased planning and effort and thus increase the likelihood of detection.)

Interior

Employee entry can be achieved by keyed or electronic access. Policies should restrict the practice of blocking open exterior doors or allowing un-known persons to enter the building through any door other than the main entrance. If a door other than the main door must remain unlocked, the door should be observable.

Electronic security, alarms, and CCTV are effective but can be expen-sive. Alarms should be monitored systems with protocols detailing the use and the process by which to notify authorities in the event of an alarm or other emergency. Cameras should be visible, not covert. Signage should notify visitors that they are or may be under surveillance. If possible, CCTV monitoring should be installed at the main desk. CCTV/video provides digital recording and is more stable and lower maintenance than tape recordings (no tapes to change).

If possible, install a panic switch at the main desk that can be activated without attracting attention but will not be set off by accident. Use security evaluations to study areas that are weak points, areas of concern, or areas that are not observable and use the evaluation to direct security changes in those areas.

Develop and implement a visitor reporting policy. Use posted signage to inform all visitors to first check in at the school office and provide all visitors with a "visitor's badge" to allow other staff and students to know that they have signed in and are authorized to move about the building. Require all staff to wear identification badges.

Staff Behavior and Human Activity

The broken window theory also works in reverse. If people who are engaged in healthy and appropriate behavior feel safe in an area, more people who have similar interests will be drawn to the area. If these people do not feel safe there, they will not continue to occupy it.

Conversely, if people who are engaged in unhealthy or delinquent activity do not feel secure in doing so in a particular area of operation, they will move on to an area that tolerates their behavior. CPTED suggests that the less often an illegal or unhealthy behavior is challenged or reported by responsible people in an area, the more frequently that behavior will occur. To address this principle, CPTED suggests putting safe activities in unsafe areas.

For example, consider a school that has a problem area in the commons section of the building, where a group of students with gang affiliations have regularly starting loitering and intimidating the other students. The majority of the activity occurs at lunchtime. Graffiti has started appearing on the walls and benches in this area, and other students are fearful of using the vending machines or spending time at the tables. The school is reluctant to make this area off-limits because that would punish all students and defeat the purpose of having a commons area. Using the CPTED principle, the school plans for each school club to have, on a rotating basis, an information and sign-up opportunity in the commons area at noon each day. A table and chairs are placed very near the problem area. The first week, the Varsity Club members, along with their faculty advisor, are at the table during the lunch hour. The following week, members of the Radio Club, along with their faculty advisor, occupy the table. The presence of these responsible people, and the safety provided by the faculty advisor, will draw more students into the commons area and will essentially reclaim this "territory."

When applying this strategy, it is important to first make sure that the safe activity stays safe (thus the presence of the faculty advisor) and to continue to monitor the unsafe activity and then stop it from relocating to another area.

Challenge behavior is another means of establishing ownership of an environment. Encourage staff to make eye contact (called challenge behavior) with visitors as an indicator of how much ownership they and students feel for their school. A staff person or student who approaches a visitor and asks, "Can I help you?" is actually making the statement, "I belong here and I don't know you," or even asking the question "What are you doing here?"

When staff feels safe and "at home" in their surroundings, they feel comfortable making eye contact with a guest or an unknown visitor. The less secure the staff are in their surroundings, or the more bizarre the look or behavior of the visitor, the more likely the staff will ignore the visitor or look away (avoidance behavior). Another less direct example of challenge behavior is staring. Staring sends several messages: "I see you, I don't know you, and I'm watching what you are doing."

Security Department or Team

A security team can be in-house, trained and licensed professionals, professional contracted security, or untrained staff identified and "willing" to help manage threatening situations. Security team members should patrol the building, randomly check doors, check in with the main desk personnel and administrators, and check on vulnerable locations or staff. They should be as nondisruptive and nonintrusive as possible. As an added deterrent, security officers should be highly visible and professional in appearance.

PERSONAL SAFETY: DEALING WITH ANGRY PEOPLE

It is quite natural to feel uncomfortable or intimidated when we are around a person who is angry or aggressive. Our self-defense mechanisms recognize these behaviors as a potential threat and will start taking our mind and body into a mode of behavior often referred to as "flight, fight, or freeze." As our level of anxiety grows, adrenaline and blood get pumped into our major muscle groups to provide maximum output and impact. Blood vessels and muscles that are not needed for either fighting or fleeing will decrease in their size and function, causing fine-motor dexterity to be lost or diminished. Outward signs might include trembling (shaking) or rapid breathing, and our facial complexion may significantly grow pale.

While these are obvious signs of fear, it is a mistake to associate fear with cowardice. Fear is a naturally occurring mechanism when confronted with a potential threat. Had our ancestors been without this mechanism, we would likely not be here. While cowardice is caused by fear, fear is certainly not cowardice. Associating the two is harmful and inaccurate. Just as being exposed to money does not make a person a thief, feeling fear does not make a person a coward. Feeling fear in these situations is normal; learning to control it stops it from further elevating its undesired effects.

At some point in their career, most school staff encounter hostile, angry, or aggressive people. Some positions, like assistant principals or disciplinarians, are frequently confronted by hostile students and even parents. Fear combined with the unknown (not having a plan) can exacerbate a provocative situation and turn it into a crisis. Preparing for potential aggression is the first step toward avoiding it or handling it appropriately if it occurs. The following are some considerations for interactions with angry and hostile people:

- Control, if possible, when and where the contact will occur: If confronted by an angry employee, adult or student, attempt to pause the situation and reschedule a time to meet, even if it is ten or fifteen minutes later. By doing so, it is easier to be better prepared emotionally and have time to collect information to better address their issue. Ideally an office should be designed with a buffer or gateway so that an angry person cannot directly enter without challenge. Also consider providing office staff with physical and psychological barriers for angry visitors. This can be done using a cabinet and counter, half wall, or simply arranging desks or plants as barriers between staff and the public. (See also bullet point "Prepare Ahead of Time.")
- Determine their issue: Their underlying issue may not always be readily apparent. Dissatisfaction and disagreement will often be euphemized as a generalization or a benign issue, and thus the anger may seem incongruent. For example, a parent may be angry that his son is not the starting quarterback on the football team but may begin his confrontation by saying, "I'm tired of the way you guys are running this school." While he may be embarrassed to confess his real issue, his stated issue cannot be resolved until this underlying issue is determined.
- Avoid the temptation of responding in kind: Professional status is an advantage. Don't surrender advantage by resorting to unprofessional behavior such as ridicule or sarcasm. Instead, regulate speech and body language to be nonaggressive and nonconfrontational in appearance. On the other hand, while showing concern and empathy, be careful not to appear so concerned that it becomes disingenuous. Treat the person first, then the

problem. Allowing them to vent their anxiety or express their dissatisfaction may be what they need to do as a way of avoiding further agitation.

- Acknowledge their issue and validate their feelings: Listen to what they have to say and hear them out; ignoring them or minimizing their feelings will tend to further escalate their anger. Many workplace incidents of aggression could have been averted had supervisors or managers listened with empathy to disgruntled employees rather than responding in an insensitive or uncaring manner. Once again consider body language. Be present and accessible.
- Never argue with someone when they are intoxicated: Reason, logic, and communication skills will likely be wasted. Additionally, the effects of the alcohol can create a Dr. Jekyll and Mr. Hyde personality that will have the visitor sobbing and remorseful one minute and aggressively angry the next. Call local law enforcement if they are not responsive to redirection and boundaries and also if they will be driving when they leave the facility.
- Allow everyone involved to physically escape the situation: Don't block anyone's way or prevent egress, as such attempts can cause a dangerous situation. Furthermore, keep personal escape paths open and the environment accessible to help.
- Prepare ahead of time: Give thought to the physical design of the office or meeting room. Consider items that can be used as weapons and eliminate them from reach. Consider developing a signal to support staff in case assistance is needed.
- Don't try to solve an emotional issue with logical arguments: Trying to defuse an angry person with evidence of their thinking errors usually makes a situation worse. Do not overwhelm someone who is emotional with facts to the contrary or reasons for why they shouldn't feel the way they do or why they should feel differently. Keep statements simple and calm, while acknowledging their argument and concern.

OTHER ASSESSMENT PROTOCOLS

A school may also develop and implement protocols for the screening of suicide and fire setting as well as the management of sexual incidents. One way of doing this is to use the same two-level system employed within the student threat assessment system (site-based assessment and community collaborative consultation) along with protocols that have investigative questions written to accurately assess the issue of concern. In other words, the protocol for suicide assessment should contain questions and an investigation process that focuses specifically on suicide risk. The same applies to fire-setting and sexual incidents.

The strength of STAS is that it was developed from a variety of perspectives, including education, mental health, social work, and law enforcement in both rural and metropolitan regions. It is the expertise and diversity of those perspectives that can be applied to other areas of potentially detrimental behaviors (e.g., suicide, sexual misconduct, and fire setting).

The STAS protocol is designed for use with the category of students who are engaged in circumstances that suggest the potential for aggression directed at other people. It is not designed for use with students who are categorically suicidal, acting out sexually, or who are setting fires, unless they are doing so as an act of extreme aggression (violence) intending severe or lethal injury to others.

Assessment protocols that are designed for specific risk concerns should not be used to assess other risk concerns for which the protocol was not designed. For example, fire setting would not be adequately assessed by violence threat assessment unless the act of fire setting was orchestrated to harm or target others.

In the same way, violence threat assessment itself would not adequately or effectively screen for suicide risk. However, if a student is exhibiting aggressive behavior and they are also reporting thoughts of suicide, a parallel assessment process would be warranted. A STAS model should include prompts in the site-based assessment that would suggest the need of a separate but parallel site-based suicide risk assessment.

Another potential misuse of a violence threat assessment protocol is employing it to assess the risk of sexualized behaviors. Sexualized behaviors can be acts of aggression but more frequently can be a sign of sexual misconduct or other at-risk behaviors. A specific two-level model can identify normative or developmentally appropriate sexual behavior or behavior that is nonnormative or indicative of predatory behavior. The presence of these types of at-risk behaviors warrants very different responses that would not be adequately addressed by the use of a violence threat assessment protocol.

Similarly, it is likely impossible to create a protocol that is generic to all detrimental behaviors without sacrificing the clarity of risk factors specific to a categorical issue of concern (such as suicide) and thus fall short of the best steps for intervention. A well-designed protocol provides an inquiry that accurately attends to the at-risk behavior and provides intervention and supervision strategies appropriate to the situation, including a move to further assessment.

To further illustrate, suicidal ideation, for example, would best be addressed using the assessment questions recommended by experts and a protocol that is conducted by trained professionals. In the state of Oregon, suicide is the second-leading cause of death among ten- to twenty-four-year-olds. In a given day, educators are often the only professionals interacting with students who are experiencing depression or suicidal ideation. Even the most seasoned educators can be rattled by the disclosure that a student is despondent and contemplating suicide.

To understand the ideation and the risk, the professional doing the assessment must be able to determine whether the idea is the fleeting thought of a student experiencing a level of distress, a call for help by a student without the skills, or an authentic disclosure of an evolving plan that is progressing toward a tragic end. Clearly each of these scenarios warrants very different intervention, yet only a small percentage of professional educators have the experience, skill set, and confidence to be the sole triage person.

A two-level suicide risk protocol can assist educators by putting handles on what can be a scary and convoluted situation. A well-designed site-based assessment protocol can provide a confident prescription for further Level 2 assessment as well as other interventions. In addition to the benefits of shared liability, the intervention's effectiveness is strengthened by examining risky behavior through a multidisciplinary lens rather than a single-examiner lens.

Without a system with specially designed protocols, school staff may find themselves underidentifying students in need of intensive crisis services. Conversely, schools can be creating excessive alarm if they do not have the correct tools to adequately and effectively examine the at-risk behavior. Without a system, educators are left to second-guess their judgment or operate in isolation, bearing the weight of decisions regarding life-and-death risk factors. The swift identification of a suicidal youth and the application of appropriate intervention can ultimately save lives.

To summarize, school personnel, specifically building counselors and administrators, are regularly presented with issues of student misconduct and at-risk behavior. The challenge is to quickly assess the nature of the infraction, the severity of the behavior, whom to involve for investigative or consultative support, and how to determine the best course of action to decrease the risk. This challenge is best met with a system that addresses at-risk behaviors with specific protocols but within a common two-level system.

Using a common system establishes a familiarity that leads to both confidence and best practice. Within the system, it is critical that the emphasis is placed on the merit of the team process. No single individual should bear the weight of assessing or managing high-risk behaviors, nor should a single individual be responsible for implementing and monitoring plans for safety and supervision. In addition, the allocation of responsibilities cannot solely fall on schools. Schools must partner with parents and local community agencies to maximize our efforts and accomplishments.

The team-based decision making and supervision planning is critical for an accurate needs assessment and the appropriate design of intervention and safety planning, regardless of the risk category. In addition, STAS and other two-level systems can formalize exceptional collaborative community teams comprising schools, law enforcement, public mental health, juvenile justice systems, and other social service agencies where there is shared ownership, responsibility, and liability.

When such programs are effectively implemented, the outcome is the increase of monitoring and the addition of protective factors along with well-designed intervention and supervision that can decrease agitating factors in the school, home, and community. These systems have had proven success in large urban centers in addition to demonstrating success in rural communities with limited resources.

While this chapter is only a cursory examination of a school's many safety issues, it may serve as a starting point for review and improvement. Further information regarding protocols, recommendations, and application can be obtained through Salem-Keizer Public Schools (contact information provided within this manual) or through the other references noted.

Chapter Eleven

Adult Threat Assessment

Dave Okada, Rod Swinehart, John Van Dreal,
Darling Mendoza, Allan Rainwater, Ray Byrd

Youth violence is just one aspect of community violence. In addition to a student threat assessment team, a community should establish a team to address adult threats such as workplace violence (including the adult personnel in schools), threats to public figures, domestic violence, and stalking. Smaller communities or communities with few resources may want to create one team that addresses both youth and adult threats, as the two teams do operate in similar fashion; however, it is important to note that most adult threat assessment teams are primarily advisory and consultative in function, since the bulk of the assessment work has often been done by the agency presenting the case to the team.

This chapter is a brief introduction to adult threat assessment and the importance of an adult threat assessment or advisory team. It is divided into three sections. The first section surveys the details of a multiagency assessment and advisement team; the second addresses domestic violence, a chronic community problem (and the behavior most frequently addressed by an adult team); and the third addresses workplace violence—less common, but a behavior with considerable potential for immediate and severe impact on a community.

ADULT THREAT ASSESSMENT, MANAGEMENT, AND THE ADULT THREAT ADVISEMENT TEAM

An adult assessment team should be multidisciplinary and composed of, but not limited to, law enforcement agencies (including domestic violence prevention teams), the district attorney's office, government and court security staff, public mental health departments, and education institutions (K-12 school districts as well as higher education). The team is actually more of a Level 2 "advisory" team, providing consultation to its membership agencies regarding the cases they bring for staffing.

The team encourages agency members to complete an assessment (the equivalent of a Level 1 assessment) prior to bringing a case to the table for staffing; thus, the majority of the assessment takes place within the field, by law enforcement, the district attorney's investigators, mental health professionals, domestic violence intervention professionals, or other public service professionals who encounter and manage risk. It should be noted that, unlike the student threat assessment system Level 1, a formal initial assessment process is not necessary, but set procedures are helpful.

The focus of the team is the prevention of targeted acts of violence by adult members of the community. Through the cooperative sharing of information, resources, experience, and the knowledge gained through training with leading experts in the field of threat assessment, the team identifies and manages situations where the risk of violence is anticipated or imminent. Threat assessment and management begins when one of the following triggering events are present:

- A threat
- An inappropriate communication
- The execution and issuance of a restraining or stalking order
- A report of suspicious activity
- The recognition of preincident indicators of violence

The above-listed areas of concern may not always be cause for a full, Level 2 threat assessment; however, each situation should be examined according to its situational uniqueness with a focus on significant changes in behavioral patterns or other situational factors that could aggravate the situation.

The team does not manage or investigate cases. Control of the case always remains with the presenting agency. As with student threat assessment, adult assessment and consultation focuses on situations involving people and does not isolate an individual through profiling or psychological evaluation. Confidentiality standards are strictly maintained while public health and safety are always the foremost concern.

In communities with limited resources, the establishment of one team may adequately handle both adult cases and youth cases; however, the differences in risk factors, management resources, and legal/educational complications must be recognized and considered. In communities where the two teams function separately, there will remain a prominent overlap in their membership, as the work involves specialized training and skills that can be applied to both teams.

In addition to the overlap in staff, both teams will share cases. When staffing adult domestic violence, it is common that involved children are affected in school, often acting out aggressively with peers or teachers. Protective orders resulting from domestic violence may also contain custody information that is important to schools. Thus, both teams review cases in common.

As with the student threat assessment team, the adult threat advisory team uses information sources to funnel information from the community to a single contact (a member of the team). Using relationships and networking within the community systems, members of the team pursue resources and build management plans. Short-term planning is essential in decreasing immediate risk, while long-term planning is often needed to decrease the risk of violence in the future (Corcoran and Cawood, 2003).

The following is a list of options to consider when staffing adult cases. It is intended only to provide ideas and is not to be viewed as comprehensive or complete:

- Watch, wait, and monitor
- Third-party intervention
- Intervention interview
- Administrative action
- Protective orders
- Mental health commitment
- Arrest
- Public safety overrides
- Bail increase
- Red flag for prosecution
- Red flag for courts
- Enhanced sentencing
- Release conditions for probation
- Safety planning
- Psychological evaluations
- Access to social services
- Mental health referrals
- Shift targets
- "Harden" targets
- Law enforcement contact as "knock and talk"
- Placing pressure through contact with peripherally involved people

As an example of a functioning adult threat advisement team, the Marion County Threat Advisory Team or TAT has been in existence for over a decade and currently meets weekly (at a minimum). The team is somewhat of an institution within the community and is frequently used by government officials, court personnel, law enforcement, mental health agencies, and education institutions. Its membership currently is:

- Marion County Sheriff's Office
- Salem Police Department
- Oregon State Police
- Keizer Police Department
- Marion County District Attorney's Office
- Salem-Keizer School District
- Willamette Educational Service District
- Marion County Health Department

In addition to the above, the team has consultation members from Oregon's Veteran's Affairs Hospital, Western Oregon University, Willamette University, and Chemeketa Community College.

The following are a few rules established for team operation:

- The team does not manage cases.
- The team does not investigate cases.
- Control of the case remains with the presenting agency.
- All members have equal status, regardless of rank.
- The team is advisory only; thus, the team does not generate reports.
- The team does not assess people; it assesses situations.
- The team does not profile.
- The team maintains confidentiality within its structure.
- Each member operates under their agency's confidentiality rules.

DOMESTIC VIOLENCE

Domestic violence can be identified as a pattern of abusive behavior within a relationship by one partner against the other in order to gain and maintain power and control. The majority of cases that reach the threat assessment team involve an abusive male partner; therefore, for the sake of simplicity, this text will use the masculine pronoun as the generic perpetrator descriptor and the feminine pronoun as descriptor of the victim.

However, female abusers certainly do exist, within many diverse relationships and situations (opposite-sex relationships, same-sex relationships, parent-child relationships, and child-parent relationships). Domestic violence can happen to anyone, regardless of race, religion, culture, economic status, and/or level of education. Abuse includes but is not limited to verbal, physical, emotional, psychological, economic, and/or sexual.

Although an abuser may not use a level of physical or sexual abuse that leaves physical evidence, such as broken bones or bruises, the abuse may be considered severe to the victim and thus leave emotional scars. Survivors coping with abuse must be offered support and resources to help them heal and decrease the impact the abuse may have on their decision-making skills and relationships.

A survivor of domestic violence cannot be blamed for the abuse and must receive nonjudgmental support for her situation. If a victim feels supported, it is more likely that she will participate in taking the steps necessary to make her offender accountable. If a victim chooses not to cooperate in the process of holding her offender accountable, it is safe to assume that she considers the repercussions to be too risky.

The situation defines the level of community intervention (from victim support to perpetrator arrest and incarceration) and rarely offers guarantees; therefore, the victim ultimately decides whether the consequences are worth her personal involvement in offender accountability. Assisting a survivor in safety and healing can be done with or without their participation in offender accountability. Those assessing or supporting victims must maintain ongoing sensitivity to the jeopardy and fear caused by an abuse experience.

It is important to encourage third parties, who are aware of possible abusive relationships with friends or colleagues, to approach the victim with support, information, and resources and thus assist her in making informed and healthy choices regarding safety. Also encourage third parties to report any immediate violent situation to authorities and the police. Any immediate intervention by authorities may save someone's life.

Coach them to heed their intuition and never dismiss their worry as overreaction. Provide a process by which concerned people can give an account and description of the behavior and actions that prompted them to notice the situation.

The following are five major warning signs of a possible abusive situation. It is a list of communication, behavior, and actions that should increase concern; however, it is not intended to be a complete list:

- *Charm.* Abusers can be very charming. In the beginning, they may seem to be almost unbelievably charming and caring. They can be very engaging, thoughtful, considerate, and charismatic. They may use that charm to gain very personal information about their victim, and they will use that information later for advantage.
- *Isolation.* Abusers isolate their victims geographically and socially. Geographic isolation includes moving the victim from her or his friends, fam-

ily, and support system (often hundreds of miles) and moving frequently in the same area and/or relocating to a rural area. Social isolation usually begins with a gradual domination of the victim's time, eventually isolating the victim from family, friends, and coworkers. Eventually, the victim is isolated from anyone who may be a possible support.

- *Jealousy.* Jealousy is a tool abusers use to control the victim. They constantly accuse the victim of having affairs or inappropriate relationships with others such as coworkers, business contacts, or even casual acquaintances.
- *Emotional Abuse.* The goal of emotional abuse is to destroy the victim's self-esteem. The abuse may take the form of blaming the victim for the violence she receives, put-downs and harsh or irrational criticism, derogatory names, labels, or direct insults. The emotional abuse may also occur as ongoing direct threats or veiled threats (such as references to violent acts committed by others or statements such as "it would be unfortunate if you fell down the stairs or slipped in the shower"). Over time, the victim no longer believes she deserves to be treated with respect and begins to blame herself for the violence. For some survivors of domestic violence, recovery from the emotional abuse may be more difficult than the recovery from the physical abuse.
- *Control.* This is the ultimate goal of the abuser. In time, the abuser will control every aspect of the victim's life: where she goes, her hairstyles, clothing choices, and relationships with others. The abuser will control the money and most, if not all, of the family's decisions. Abusers are also very controlled people. While they appear to go into a rage or be out of control, they are very much in control of their behavior. And while they may blame external causes for their behavior (such as drugs and alcohol), the choice to act out in an abusive manner remains within their control.

Domestic violence does not only affect the direct victim. Abusers are often falsely perceived by their victim and other family members and friends as good fathers to their children or stepchildren. Of course, a good parent does not abuse a child's loved one (parent); furthermore, children are usually very aware of what happens in their home and are in many ways affected by it.

Abusers might choose to be directly violent with their children by physically or emotionally hurting them and exerting control over the household (food, entertainment, activity) and may offer unreasonable punishment by calling it "discipline." The abuser can also use the children as an instrument of coercion, telling the victim that she will never see them again or threatening to hurt her in front of them if she resists or informs. Children may also be affected by custody battles in which the abuser forces or entices the children into visitation with him in order to complicate the life of his victim.

In situations involving children, use the threat advisement process to inform school staff of the situational dynamics and organize resources to minimize the impact. Informing school staff also adds a deterrent for the offender, as he will know the situation is being monitored.

Consider counseling and emotional support to children who have been a part of the abuse cycle, as they are at higher risk for behavioral problems, social conflict, and academic failure. Contrary to popular belief, children are able to survive abuse by learning to make positive choices that will benefit and not harm their future, allowing them to thrive as adults and stopping the cycle of violence.

Domestic violence can also be identified in dating relationships among adolescents. Abusers don't suddenly become abusive in their adult years; it is a process in which an abuser identifies that being abusive will accomplish a goal (usually control through power or forced companionship) and views it as acceptable behavior. Thus, it is extremely important to provide early intervention in teen dating violence by teaching the young abuser the undesired consequences of violent behavior and by preventing the victim from normalizing the behavior.

Within their environment, teen abusers use the same tactics as adult abusers to gain and maintain power and control over their dating partner. Teen dating violence should not be dismissed as "kids being kids"; it should rather be seen as a serious, if not potentially fatal, situation. Without intervention, a teen abuser learns he can get away with abusive behavior and may ultimately choose to escalate his behavior because he has come to feel entitled and because his behavior has not caused him enough undesired consequence.

WORKPLACE VIOLENCE

Workplace violence can occur in many forms. It can stem from a domestic violence situation continued at the workplace, or it can generate from disgruntled employee relations. It can also occur as a result of customer relations or a number of other mixed dynamics within the workplace.

As with domestic violence or any situation causing concern, encourage people to always report to authorities and the police any suspicion or concern regarding a possible violent situation. Encourage them to act on their intuition and not dismiss their worry as overreaction. Have them proceed with an account and description of the behavior and actions that prompted them to notice the situation.

The following is a list of communication, behavior, and actions that should increase concern; however, it is not intended to be a complete list:

- Overwhelmingly or unbearably stressful experiences with an indication of a limited ability to cope; a noted lack of alternatives to aggressive or violent action (de Becker, 1998)
- Noted justification and motive for harm or violent action (de Becker, 1998)
- The intellectual and mental capacity to act out in a premeditated manner; the expressed ability to be violent and seek revenge (de Becker, 1998)
- An expressed interest in possible targets, including particular, identifiable targets
- Strange, awkward, or intimidating communication with potential targets
- Consideration and/or attempt to harm self or others
- Attempt to secure or the securing and possession of weapons; practice with weapons or the use of weapons (or proxy weapons) as a rehearsal/simulation of a violent act
- Following, stalking, or the approach of potential targets, either with or without weapons, at events, occasions, or in private
- The stated or implied acceptance of the consequences from acting out in a violent manner (de Becker, 1998)

This chapter is supplemental information to assist schools in considering a system that includes the assessment of adult threats. It is not intended to fully identify all adult threat risk factors and assessment principles or to fully outline a system for adult threat assessment and management. For further information, use the information within this manual to contact members of the Marion County Adult Threat Advisement Team or pursue the noted references.

Chapter Twelve

Threat Assessment in Higher Education

John Van Dreal, Martin Speckmaier

Campuses of higher education (postsecondary) have certainly been targets for campus rampage shootings. Furthermore, community colleges, universities, and other colleges also experience situations of workplace violence and domestic violence. Thus, higher-education security departments should consider a threat assessment and management system that is timely, effective, and defensible.

Unfortunately, the preattack behaviors demonstrated by college campus attackers have not been thoroughly examined; thus, current available recommendations are based on combinations of risk factors taken from the Safe School Initiative and studies on the adult perpetrators of targeted violence such as domestic violence, workplace violence, and attacks on public officials.

Using the Safe School Initiative findings may provide reasonable insight to guide higher-education threat assessment teams; however, there are many differences between the college setting and the K-12 setting to consider (diversity, physical environment, communication and tracking of student issues, loss of familiarity with student's personal or behavioral concerns, the presence of the residential situation, and the transitional issues associated with the move toward adulthood, loss of family support, etc.; Drysdale et al., 2010).

In fact, the violence in higher-education settings seems to be quite similar to the violence in the greater community. Therefore, this chapter is not intended to provide everything needed for a complete system but is the starting point for those in higher education to use and adapt.

It seems reasonable to start the design by using the K-12 student threat assessment system outlined in this book and then adapt the design to best fit higher-education campus needs, using the available writings and recommendations of experts in adult threat assessment and higher-education campus threat assessment. Again, it is only a starting point and should be considered a basic template at best, until a more complete and definitive protocol is available.

In 1990 the Jeanne Clery Disclosure of Campus Security Policy and Campus Crime Statistics Act, commonly referred to as the Clery Act, was enacted for postsecondary institutions. The single most important aspect of the Clery Act is that postsecondary institutions are required to provide timely warning of threats—in other words, campus administrators have a duty to warn and to protect their students from crime and violence.

Since the Clery Act also recommends a case-by-case assessment of the facts regarding threatening situations, most institutions will find it necessary to coordinate these compliance activities not only with the many offices throughout the campus, but also with those external community stakeholders with protective responsibilities.

Those with protective responsibilities are to be defined within their school policy as a "School Official with Legitimate Educational Interest," and the Clery Act further defines that criteria as "any person who has the authority and the duty to take action or respond to particular issues on behalf of the institution" and extends to "contractors, consultants, and others who work with a college of school" (*Inside Higher Ed.*, March 24, 2008). Selecting internal and external community stakeholders for the threat assessment team is critical to the success of a campus threat assessment team.

College campus threat assessment team members identify, assess, and manage threatening situations. Because most threatening situations are multifaceted and complex, team members must possess certain character traits. As noted in previous chapters, the membership should consist of professionals with the following attributes (Fein, 2002):

- A reputation within the school campus and the community for fairness and trustworthiness
- Discretion and an appreciation for the importance of keeping information confidential, of the possible harm that may result in the inappropriate release of information
- Cognizance of the difference between harming and helping in an intervention
- A questioning, analytical, and skeptical mindset
- Training in the collection and evaluation of information from multiple sources
- Familiarity with childhood and adolescent growth and development, the campus environment, the need for safe schools, and the community
- An ability to relate well to staff, colleagues, other professionals, students, parents, and others
- Credibility, respect, and strong interpersonal skills

• The ability to serve as a formal link or liaison between various systems and meet regularly with them; to be a "connector" and "boundary spanner"

Additionally, team members should have the authority and ability to make decisions within their area or expertise, with the diplomatic skills to explain the system and inform others of its availability.

It's important to understand that the Clery Act's recommendations are a "minimum standard." It's only telling postsecondary education what must be done and does not limit the options for exceeding the requirements.

FERPA (Family Education Rights to Privacy Act) is also an important consideration when putting together a campus threat assessment team. FERPA specifically states "information from education records may be shared with police, social services, or other community representatives who are serving on a school's established threat assessment committee, if they are school officials with legitimate educational interests in accordance with school's established criteria" (FERPA 34 CFR 99.3 and (b) 99.8).

If they have not already done so, college campuses should establish a law enforcement unit record. FERPA only applies to "education records," which means records, files, and documents. FERPA does not protect the confidentiality of information in general; it protects information from education records only (FERPA/34 CFR 99.3, (b) 99.8).

FERPA excludes from the definition of education records a school's law enforcement unit's records. A law enforcement unit record (LEU) is an individual, office, department, division, or other component of an educational agency or institution that is officially authorized or designated by that agency or institution to enforce any local, state, or federal law or refer to appropriate authorities a matter for enforcement of any local, state, federal law…or to maintain the physical security and safety of the agency or institution (20 U.S.C. 1232g(a)(4)(B)(ii)/FERPA 99.8).

This means that institutions of higher learning may formalize a threat assessment team process and thus share certain information from education records with members of that team for the purposes of identifying, assessing, and managing threatening or potentially threatening situations. That information now becomes part of the LEU, which is exempt from the constraints of sharing of information under FERPA.

Furthermore, the U.S. Secret Service and Department of Education encourage threat assessment teams to identify opportunities for including threatening situations in schools as exceptions to constraints on the disclosure of information contained in education records (Fein, 2002). This means that college campus teams are not only obligated to share information regarding a potential "Virginia Tech" shooter, they are encouraged to share information regarding those unique situations that have been identified as threats in the community (e.g., gangs and/or potential gang members).

In September of 2007 the National Association of Attorneys General released their report and recommendations from the Task Force on School and Campus Safety. Among the campus safety procedures promoted, they stressed that all schools and colleges should establish a system whereby disturbing behavior is reported to an individual or team of individuals with expertise and training that can assess the information received and take action when appropriate (threat assessment teams).

In June of 2007 "The Report to the President on Issues Raised by the Virginia Tech Tragedy" was released by the Department of Education, Department of Health and Human Services, and the Department of Justice. The five key suggestions were:

• Eliminate perceived obstacles to information sharing.
• Keep guns out of the wrong hands.
• Improve awareness and communication.
• Secure mental illness service for those who need it.
• Where we know what to do, we have to get better at doing it through practice and effective communication.

The Virginia Tech Report recommendations also stressed the importance of creating interdisciplinary teams to evaluate information regarding threats, assess the degree of threat, and intervene to preempt the threat (again, threat assessment teams).

Threat assessment teams should meet regularly, even if there are no situations of concern at the time of the meeting, because, as the last key finding from above reminds us, "where we know what to do, we have to get better at doing it through practice and effective communication."

The adage "Even if you're on the right track, you'll get run over if you just sit there" accurately summarizes what may happen if we allow a team process to become stagnant. Conducting a facilitated meeting once a week for an hour is highly recommended. By hand-selecting team members based on the above attributes and meeting regularly we can help assure that the team process stays active, effective, and sustainable!

As teams develop and determine their course, they can develop protocols for assessment based upon the risk factors identified in previous chapters and the material noted in the bibliography. Below is an adaptation of the K-12 system already outlined in this book as it may apply to postsecondary education. The investigative questions list is only a partial list and does not include factors specific to domestic violence or workplace violence.

As noted earlier, aggression is a feature of basic human behavior and is a survival trait possessed by all people capable of basic functioning, regardless of their age, development, or cognitive ability. In other words, all humans have the capacity to act out violently given the right circumstances (de Becker, 1998). Therefore, the students and staff within a higher education campus would likely fit within the same kind of investigation as other groups or populations of people.

If indicated, domestic violence and workplace violence assessment tools should be reviewed in conjunction with the investigative questions focusing on targeted campus violence (noted below). Information on domestic violence and workplace violence is available in chapter 11 or through the resources noted within this manual.

SYSTEM

The following is an adaptation of the student threat assessment system outlined in chapter 5. It is designed with a two-tier process that requires a Level 1 team that is site based on the campus and a Level 2 team that is community based. For large university campuses with community-like resources (law enforcement, mental health), it can be adapted to include the Level 2 team as a campus-based team while the Level 1 teams can function within individual colleges or departments.

The system illustrated in figures 12.1 and 12.2 is initiated through an act of violence or implied threat of violence. If imminent danger exists, notify law enforcement and the security department and initiate a protective response using the institution's guidelines.

Information collected through the Level 1 assessment is then considered by members of the campus team. The Level 1 assessment is recommended for investigation and documentation of concerns about dangerous student activities, behaviors, statements, other communication, or ideation. A direct threat (expressed or acted out) does not have to be clearly indicated in order to proceed with a Level 1 assessment. Campus teams are encouraged to use the Level 1 assessment to address concerns and document their review of potential danger or safety issues, even if dismissed as minor or unlikely.

The Level 1 assessment process can be used as a reasonably short (twenty- to thirty-minute) review or a more extensive and lengthy assessment (depending upon the circumstances). The assessment is completed by the campus team.

- The campus team includes an administrator, student services staff, a counselor or mental health professional, a police officer, and security staff. In-

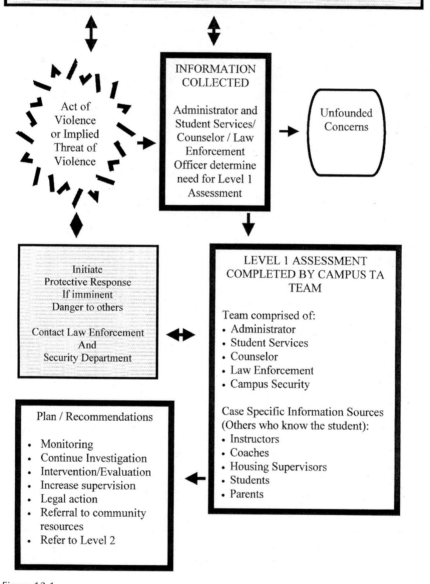

Law Enforcement (Criminal Investigation, Custody, Adjudication, Referral, Release). Ongoing information sharing between Law Enforcement and Threat Assessment Process

Act of Violence or Implied Threat of Violence

INFORMATION COLLECTED

Administrator and Student Services/ Counselor / Law Enforcement Officer determine need for Level 1 Assessment

Unfounded Concerns

Initiate Protective Response If imminent Danger to others

Contact Law Enforcement And Security Department

LEVEL 1 ASSESSMENT COMPLETED BY CAMPUS TA TEAM

Team comprised of:
• Administrator
• Student Services
• Counselor
• Law Enforcement
• Campus Security

Case Specific Information Sources (Others who know the student):
• Instructors
• Coaches
• Housing Supervisors
• Students
• Parents

Plan / Recommendations

• Monitoring
• Continue Investigation
• Intervention/Evaluation
• Increase supervision
• Legal action
• Referral to community resources
• Refer to Level 2

Figure 12.1

structors, coaches, housing supervisors, students, parents, and others who know the student/s of concern should be included as information sources.

- Using the Level 1 student threat assessment (see below), the site team addresses risk factors and management needs through an investigation and subsequent supervision/intervention plan (included in the Level 1 student assessment). The case is tracked and case managed by members of the campus team. Follow-up dates are scheduled as needed. Law enforcement pursues a criminal investigation if indicated.
- Document all notification and safeguards. Provide safety plans for students, staff, or community members who have been identified as possible targets or victims.

If the campus Level 1 team determines that outside resources need to be explored or further consultation and advisement are necessary, contact the community or Level 2 threat advisement team (if one exists) or any regional threat assessment expertise available through law enforcement. Community threat advisory teams or Level 2 (see figure 12.2) teams are composed of representatives from law enforcement, school districts, higher education, public mental health, justice departments, county human resources, and parole and probation departments.

Once a student or individual situation of concern is staffed, case management will continue through the campus Level 1 team and the case will be reviewed on a schedule determined at the time of the Level 2 consultation or as needed if the situation escalates. Some cases may extend through semesters and even years.

CAMPUS THREAT ASSESSMENT LEVEL 1 ASSESSMENT TOOL RECOMMENDATIONS

The following questions are adapted from the Level 1 questions noted in chapter 5. They are suggested for inclusion in a threat assessment tool (in combination with assessment tools designed for domestic violence, stalking, or workplace violence if indicated) for students, staff, and/or other individuals of concern who are engaged in circumstances that suggest the potential for targeted aggression directed at other people on higher-education campuses.

The questions are not designed for use with people who are suicidal, acting out sexually, or who are setting fires, unless they are doing so as an act of violence intended to seriously or lethally injure other people. The answers to the questions do not predict future violence, nor are they a foolproof method of assessing an individual's or group's risk of harm to others.

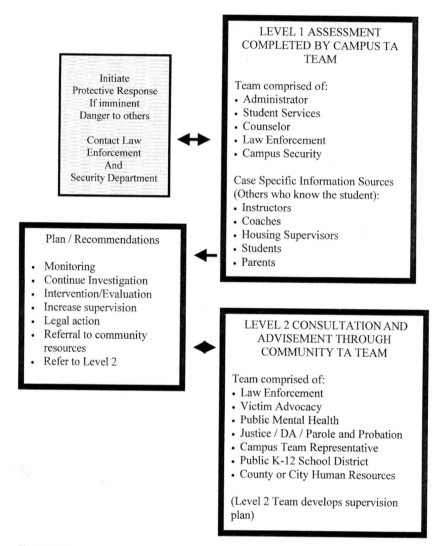

Figure 12.2

The questions do not make up a checklist that can be quantified. They are a guide designed to assist in the investigation of potential danger (to identify circumstances and variables that may increase risk for potential targeted aggression or violence) and to assist the campus staff in the development of a safety and management plan.

1. Define the threat, behavior, or dangerous situation using the aggression continuum (see figure 4.1 in chapter 4). Is aggression mild (a

high-frequency but low-impact behavior such as posturing and bravado, pushing, or light hitting/kicking); moderate (infrequent but with greater impact in injury such as fistfighting or battering); or extreme (even less frequent, but impact is serious or even lethal injury such as beating, raping, stabbing, shooting, or bombing)?

This question asks for a clarification of the threat. Note that there is a change within the continuum from aggression (nonserious or nonlethal injury) to extreme aggression or what is sometimes termed as violence (serious or lethal injury). Also, while there is a suggested progression of behavior from mild to extreme, the listed examples serve only as illustration and are not necessarily locked into their position within the continuum. In other words, hitting can be a mild, moderate, or even extreme form of aggression, depending upon the intention or the outcome of harm.

2. Have there been communications suggesting a potential attack or act of aggression (such as direct threats, specific references, veiled threats, or vague warnings)?

This question addresses the type of communication indicating a threat. Threats are sometimes made directly in verbal communication, art, email, Internet use, written language exercises, and any other medium of communication. They can also be made by indirect, veiled, or casual references to possible harmful events, ominous warnings, or references to previously occurring violent events such as school, community, or family shootings.

A threat does not have to be specifically stated to be of concern, nor does it have to be stated or implied within the campus setting. Threat assessment teams should have a designated team member that regularly monitors public websites where individuals of concern may be posting intentions of violent plans and/or ideation.

3. Are there indications of a plan, feasible process, or clear intention to harm others?

This question addresses attack-related behavior. Threatening language is just language without related behavior or intent. Many threats are not stated with language but are indicated by attack-related behavior. Attack-related behavior may be, but is not limited to, the following:

- *A plan (complex or simple)* to carry out a targeted act of violence or aggression against a specific individual, group, or student body. Such a plan would have a sequence of actions necessary for its success and almost always requires a motive. The more plausible and detailed the plan, the greater the risk.
- *The acquisition of a weapon*, the attempted acquisition of a weapon, or research about how to acquire a weapon. (If the threat is the use of

physical force to the point of serious or lethal injury, then the physical force is the weapon.)

- *The rehearsal of the event or a similar event.* Rehearsal is like simulation or practice. Rehearsal or simulation is often necessary before a targeted event can be completely planned and carried out. Rehearsal can be indicated through art, fantasy games, writing or film projects, the use of movies or Internet sites that have themes and sequences of violence that allow the simulation of targeted and violent acts, or through first-person shooter video games that also allow for simulation of sequential and violent acts. However, the use of such games or movies as entertainment does not lead students to act out violently. Their use is only attack-related behavior when it becomes rehearsal or simulation and practice.
- *Scheduling an attack.* Scheduling the act is sometime indicated through communication or actually noted in clear detail. Sometimes the schedule is flexible, awaiting a triggering event (teasing, rejection, loss) that further justifies the violence and locks it in as the only solution.

4. Are there indications of suicidal ideation?

   This question examines the presence or history of suicidal ideas, gestures, references, and intent. The wish to die, be killed, or commit suicide combined with a threat to harm others increases risk, especially if the self-destructive behavior is the last part of a plan to harm others and carry out revenge or justice. If there is a risk of suicide, contact supports, counselor, or law enforcement as required by local law and policy and refer for further suicide assessment.

5. Are there indications of a specific target or a focus of aggressive or violent ideation?

   This question examines the focus of the aggression or violent ideation or behavior. Is there an ongoing consideration or focus on a particular person, group, or student body? If the situation is absent a notable target, it is likely a situation that revolves around generalized reactive aggression, used as a means to bully, intimidate, confront, or defend interests and wants.

6. Are there indications of a weapons choice and/or availability?

   This question examines a primary concern; however, it is important to remember that even if weapons are not available within the home, they are frequently available within the community.

7. Are there indications of a focused or inappropriate interest in acts of violence, previous school/community attacks or attackers, weaponry or antisocial characters, notorious criminals, murderers, or gangs (historical or fictional)?

This question is somewhat complicated. What may be inappropriate to some may still be within the normal scope of age or cultural or developmental range for others. The question is similar to #3 as it examines whether the interest is a curiosity, a fascination, or if the interest is a sort of admiration for the antisocial character as role model and example of how to justify violence as problem solving.

8. Are there indications of a motive, goal, or justification for aggressive behavior or a lethal attack?

    This question pairs with #5. If there is a focus on a specific target or targets, then there is very likely a motive. While there can certainly be many motives for acting out violently or aggressively, the most common is the need to establish or reestablish control as indicated by revenge or vendetta for lost love or humiliation and the desire to prove bravery after making a threat or taking a dare.

    If the situation is absent a motive, then it may revolve around generalized reactive aggression or the affectation of rage. Reactive aggressive and violent talk often have triggers that agitate the situation rapidly. Such triggers are usually not motives but should still be identified in order to avoid or eliminate them in the future. Examples of triggers may include stress, frustration, anxiety, or fear.

9. Are there indications of hopeless, stressfully overwhelming, or desperate situations (either real or perceived)?

    This question also examines a primary concern. As students lose hope of resolving stressful or overwhelming situations through acceptable social or coping skills, they are more likely to engage desperate solutions and last-ditch efforts to take control. It is important to note that the point of this question is to examine the perception of the person or party you are concerned with, not necessarily what is realistically observed or known by others (staff, parents, other students, or the community).

10. Are there indications of a capacity or ability to plan and carry out an act of targeted violence?

    This question examines the feasibility or possibility of a planned and carried-out threat, based upon the organizational, cognitive, or adaptive capacity of the person or party of concern. If someone is making fairly exaggerated or complex threats but is unable to organize due to supervision, cognitive ability, or overall functioning, then the feasibility decreases.

11. Are beliefs or ideas a feature of a mental health disorder?

    This question examines the presence of a mental illness as a contributing feature within the threat. Threatening talk as a feature of mental illness such as psychosis, Tourette's syndrome, or autism is often grandiose or implausible and is usually disconnected from attack-related behavior (see question #3), targeted behavior (see question #5), and even clear motive (see question #8).

Attack-related behavior, if it exists, is more quickly determined. Typically, threats that are made and are features of disabilities are less concerning than those that are made or implied with thoughtful and sober consideration that follows a process of reason and justification (social maladjustment).

12. Are actions and behaviors consistent with communications?

This question examines the relationship between communicated threats or implications of threat and the behavior that accompanies the communication. If threats are made but there is an absence of attack-related behaviors, motives, or a specific target(s) consistent with that threat, then risk decreases. Many threats that lack attack-related behavior, motives, and targets are likely to be a means of communicating dissatisfaction, attention seeking, expressing anger, releasing stress, or even an affectation of strength or power (bravado).

At this point, if any of the above questions identify a threat (actions, specific circumstances, and/or communications) that is focused on a specific target (individual or group) for a specific reason or motive and involves planning and preparation with the capacity to carry out the event, then there is an indicated risk of targeted violence. If that threat appears imminent, immediately contact law enforcement and follow the safety protocol established by the institution. If that threat does not appear imminent, the remainder of the questions will help clarify the risk.

The threat is likely a reactive or affective gesture if the responses do not indicate a targeted threat but do indicate either of the following: a threat or behavior that is a reaction of aggression or a violent idea occurring as a result of an emotional or temper outburst or as a means of defending personal interest or self; or a behavior and/or an aggressive/violent idea that is used to intimidate, bully, manipulate, or impress others.

In this case, the assessment may stop and the team should identify situations, settings, and/or triggers that agitate or increase the likelihood of the behavior and deliver increased supervision, changes in schedules, consequences, or interventions that will decrease or inhibit that behavior. If the responses indicate the absence of any threatening ideas, behavior, or circumstances, the assessment should stop but the situation should be monitored.

13. Are parents, peers, and/or campus staff concerned about a potential for acting out in a violent or aggressive way?

This question examines the concerns and opinions of others regarding the person or party of concern and the concerning situation that exists. Concerns may range from an odd discomfort to a complete list of reasons why caution should be taken. If violence is being considered or planned, it is difficult to hide the indicators. In fact, sometimes little care is actually taken to hide the intentions and, while there may be little to no documentation of past behavioral issues, there may likely be several people who have been or are currently concerned.

14. Are there trusting and successful relationships with one or more responsible adults either on campus or within the community?

This question examines the depth of relationships with prosocial adults. The greater and healthier the connection with instructors, coaches, prosocial peers, administrators, club or church leaders, and so on, the less chance there is of wanting to disappoint or hurt them.

The situation involving a marginalized student who lacks any connection to adults is often one of greater risk, as there is less to lose by acting out. This is one of the most important questions and indicators of need. If a person or group lacks connection to prosocial adults and are also marginalized within the student population, then intervention and connection is strongly indicated.

15. What circumstances, events, or triggers increase or agitate the likelihood of a violent or aggressive attack?

This question examines the obvious. If you can identify the situations that agitate or trigger violent thinking, threatening, or behavior, you can intervene and decrease the chance of a violent or aggressive incident.

16. What circumstances, events, or inhibitors decrease the likelihood of a violent or aggressive attack?

This question is similar to #15 but examines the opposite. Identify and increase actions, events, interests, relationships, goals, activities, memberships, and so on that promote responsible and accountable prosocial behavior and you can decrease the chance of a violent or aggressive incident. The situation that lacks any inhibitors is one of greater risk, as there is little to lose by acting out and little to motivate healthy solutions.

17. Are there indications that a peer group reinforces delinquent thinking? What are the relationship dynamics (leader, follower, victim, outcast, etc.)?

This question examines peer relationships, marginalization, and accepted delinquent thinking that may support using violence as a solution. Risk increases if a situation lacks positive social connection, accountability, and inhibitors but is filled with antisocial thinking about entitlement, revenge, and the use of violence as an acceptable means of solving problems.

18. Is there a history of abuse, behavioral, drug/alcohol, or developmental issues?

This question examines issues related to vulnerability and coping skills but not necessarily directly related to targeted or planned violence. Risk increases when coping skills are weak and emotional resiliency is low.

19. Are there mental health issues?

This question is similar to question #18 in that it examines an issue that may indicate a poor reserve of coping strategies and a lack of emotional resiliency.

20. Other concerns: List any other concerns. Remember that this is not a quantifiable questionnaire or a fixed checklist. It is intended as a set of pertinent questions that outline an examination of concerns and potential risk. If there are concerns with domestic violence, stalking, or workplace violence, include an investigation that addresses associated risk factors and follow notification guidelines and laws.

After the questions are discussed, a team should consider the following through team discussion:

- Review all of the previous questions and highlight/identify responses that indicate concern or risk.
- Identify your impressions and sense of urgency.
- Do the responses continue to identify threats (actions, specific circumstances, and/or communications) that are focused on a specific target (individual or group) for a specific reason or motive and involve planning and preparation with the capacity to carry out the event? If so, the risk of targeted violence continues to be indicated.
- Is there an indication of scheduling or an identified date when the attack may happen?

If the following are true, take immediate precautionary steps to protect potential victims and seek further assessment and advisement from the community-based threat advisement team (Level 2) or law enforcement:

- You have clear concerns regarding potential violence but are unable to confidently answer questions on this protocol or
- You have confidently answered the questions on this protocol and have concerns regarding threats of violence that indicated motive, plan, preparation, scheduling, and/or other behavior that suggests serious consideration of an act of targeted violence or
- You have confidently answered the questions on this protocol and have safety concerns regarding impulsive or reactive behavior that will likely result in serious or lethal injury to another.
- After completing the survey there is little indication of a threat of targeted violence; however, you and/or staff continue to have concerns regarding the safety of others and are unable to generate solutions.

PRECAUTIONARY STEPS may differ depending upon community and local laws; however, the following are examples common to most any community environment, legal boundaries, and policy options.

- Call law enforcement (campus, city, state police, or sheriff's office) and report your concerns. Identify the situation and request assistance for further threat assessment. You may also contact and engage your community collaborative threat assessment system if it exists (within local law enforcement, school district, public mental health system, human resources, etc.).
- Notify the potential target or targets. Inform them of your concerns and the actions you are initiating. Document all conversations, safety planning, and actions taken to decrease the threat.
- Consider all options available to inhibit or decrease the chances of violence. Develop a list of resources and options through your community and campus. Options may include restricting access to targets or campus; however, it is important to remember that removing students who pose a threat does not necessarily decrease that threat if they are not supervised when away from campus. Therefore, since the use of suspension or expulsion may actually increase risk, such a consequence should be factored into the risk assessment.

The following is a summary of possible options for supervision and threat management available on most campuses:

- Disciplinary action taken: If suspended, when will the student return?
- Expulsion
- Arrest and detainment
- Intended victim warned—parent/guardian notified.
- Initiate protective response
- Suicide assessment initiated through report to parent and/or law enforcement or mental health provider
- No-harm contract
- Random check-in by appointed staff
- Parents will provide supervision/intervention
- Tracking and time accountability program
- Other modifications of schedule
- Alert staff, teachers, and/or others on need-to-know basis
- Behavioral modification plan (attach copy of this report)
- Increased supervision or monitoring in designated settings
- Drug/alcohol intervention

- Review of counseling and community interventions with student/parents
- School mental health or behavioral intervention
- Assign identified staff to build relationship and connection through check-in or mentorship: administrator, mentor, counselor, teacher, other
- Provide means by which student/individual may safely report and discuss thoughts or intentions to harm others and receive appropriate intervention
- Implement interventions or supervision strategies that will directly address the identified triggers and agitators
- Identify and further develop activities, relationships, or things of value that inhibit possibility of acting out
- Referral to community threat assessment system, law enforcement, or other collaboration/agency that addresses community violence and risk; explore community resources and supervision options through consultation with community threat assessment team or other available resources

While this chapter is not complete in its recommendations and prescriptions for threat assessment in postsecondary education, it is a reasonable foundation to use as a start to designing a system. Additional elements to address domestic violence and workplace violence would likely be needed in a system that is comprehensive. Further information regarding system design and assessment can be found in the References, Additional Readings, and Resources section at the end of this book.

Chapter Thirteen

Staying Ahead of Targeted Violence

Seth G. Elliott

Since the late 1990s, the pioneering work of threat assessment teams has dramatically changed the way security is handled in schools and other public agencies. Proactive collaboration in threat assessment is working. There have been several, specific cases where plots to engage in school shootings have been stopped.

As successes multiply, the task of law enforcement, security managers, and school officials is to stay ahead of potential attackers as they attempt to adapt to the improved security systems. Doing so requires maintaining a vigilant and prevention-oriented approach along with forward thinking in both threat assessment *and* threat management capabilities.

This involves the understanding that threats will continually evolve in response to the activities of protectors. As we get better at detecting and mitigating risk, perpetrators will likely attempt to strike from creative positions of advantage and lethality that will challenge our current threat assessment and security planning. If shootings continue, we will likely see an increase in bombings, weapons variety, multiple attackers, and overall attack complexity. It is possible that off-campus but school-related events will be targeted. Would-be attackers will also learn from the cases where plots have been interrupted and uncovered, and thus improve their efforts to conceal violent plans.

In addition, the media will continue to inflate the standards of care expected by the public. Their tendency to sensationalize questions like "Why weren't schools prepared for this?" and to launch investigations of their own into preincident indicators and emerging trends creates distraction and myth and further increases our need to be proactive. Attackers will also continue to expect the media to enhance the impact of their violence with immediate national attention.

Based on these factors, we must ensure that our school threat management capabilities are as evidence-based, diverse, innovative, and legally defensible as our threat assessment capabilities. Specifically, the following areas should be continually reevaluated, adapted, and improved:

• Protective options for high-profile district administrators and board members
• Protective services and personal safety training for staff under threat of targeted violence in the workplace
• Staff training on security protocols and responses to dangerous situations
• Training for campus monitors, security, and SROs in protective strategies
• Supervision/monitoring of protective or restraining orders
• On-site physical security

It is likely that many people reading this list will envision the dollar signs piling up. However, there are ways to meet these needs in a cost-effective *and* progressive manner. As with the development of cellular phones, new and expensive technology eventually becomes the standard in the mainstream market. When cell phones were first introduced, only the very wealthy had access to them. Today cell phones are inexpensive and considered an essential tool for modern daily life. The field of threat management has evolved and, in much the same way, now includes many innovative options that were unavailable even five years ago.

This chapter introduces a few of these options for readers to consider as they look ahead to their own risk management improvement. These concepts may solve some existing situations or they may inspire even better ideas for future changes.

First of all, there are an increasing number of private protection companies that defy the historic and nightmarish stereotypes that are rightfully associated with private security. Many of these companies follow the security recommendations of international experts and have recruitment and training standards that are equal to or even exceed those of law enforcement personnel. This manual provides resources and contacts for exploring these security options to improve threat management capability.

Additionally, threat management coordinator positions have recently been added to many districts and higher-education campuses and are quickly becoming a part of the improved standard of practice. For large schools or districts, the actual follow-through on threat assessment recommendations can be a daunting task due to the number of cases that queue up for priority consideration and resources. To organize and manage the threat management function in large settings, it is advantageous to have a professional with the appropriate background to oversee the implementation and follow-through of situation monitoring, supervision, protective options, and safety planning.

Threat assessment provides a valuable preventive option, but important details for management must be attended to by a professional with both the time and the correct training. Those in this position would be free to work in a dedicated, operational role and leave other critical administrative functions to a security director or risk management director, thereby increasing the return on the investment made in funding, staffing, and running the threat assessment team.

Finally, a variety of concepts could be integrated through a protective response team (PRT)—essentially a collaborative version of the threat management coordinator. A protective response team is a group of individuals, hired as employees of school districts and/or educational service providers, who work hand in hand with threat assessment teams and security staff. PRT members must have specific training in all aspects of executive protection and have other skills and attributes that would allow them to work effectively with school personnel, law enforcement, and the community at large.

Again, the selection of these members would be based on the higher qualifications of the new paradigm of protective services, not the past field of private security. By providing close protection services, personal safety training, site security assessment, and staff training, the PRT would provide a crucial link that is currently missing between threat assessment teams and law enforcement.

Protective work is significantly different from law enforcement, but law enforcement personnel are the only ones that are currently trusted with security assignments. Unfortunately, these trusted partners in law enforcement often do not have the resources to provide a proactive, protective level of attention to just a few members of the community. Even a two- to four-person protective response team would dramatically improve the threat management and overall security posture for districts and campuses.

The positive impact of a threat management coordinator or protective response team is an exciting prospect whether staffed internally or developed through a relationship with an external partner. Consider the improvements in safety by directing trained, professional protective options to cover a superintendent speaking at a public venue during staff layoffs, or to a principal threatened with being "the first to go" as part of an imminent threat by a disgruntled parent, student, or staff member.

Furthermore, consider the option of dispatching a district member to give a presentation on personal safety planning to staff and students, or to consult with targeted individuals. Such options would greatly increase the sense of psychological safety as well as the objective level of security in a school.

The past decade of threat assessment work has taught us that being proactive matters. We can shift the focus of potential attackers, we can minimize the impact of targeted violence, and often, we can prevent it altogether. When it comes to securing our schools, we protect the most important VIPs of all. The students of today represent the public figures, celebrities, and decision makers of tomorrow. The staff that direct their education have the important task of preparing them as well as protecting them in a continuing tradition of foresight, innovation, and vigilance.

Conclusion

John Van Dreal

This manual outlines a threat assessment system that distributes responsibility and ownership among the community agencies that serve youth and is expeditious and easily initiated but still methodically utilizes the best available research and recommendations. The system uses understandable and clear terms to identify risk and intervention strategies that are fitting to the situation and accurately address safety issues. Finally, the system maintains students in school settings if possible, improving supervision and continuing education opportunity while promoting and improving the psychological sense of safety.

While it is impossible to measure events that have not occurred as a result of the student threat assessment system, it is possible to measure the opinions of those who use it. The earlier-cited 2005 study by the University of Oregon's Institute on Violence and Destructive Behavior reported that 94 percent of the administrators stated that the system effectively identified potentially dangerous students and situations; had positive effects on school safety; provided important information necessary for support, discipline, and placement decisions; and fulfilled a valuable role in schools. The same study reported that 90 percent of administrators reported that the system increased efficient coordination with law enforcement and mental health.

We cannot control all of the risks in life, but we can limit them through vigilance and appropriate prevention and response. In schools, this means creating climates of safety and respect. It means listening to our intuition, monitoring the communication flow within our schools, acting responsibly, collecting information that is concerning, and communicating and collaborating with our peers and colleagues regarding those concerns. Such efforts will greatly increase our safety and allow us to promote a safer, calmer, and more successful learning environment.

Human beings who are safe and feel safe are far more adept at teaching and learning and will experience the education process in a manner that is foundational to a successful life. This manual is an attempt at providing the structure and concepts necessary for a school campus threat assessment system; however, it can also be a blueprint for addressing many other safety and security issues. At the very least, the proposed structured multidisciplinary and multiagency collaboration would well serve any school system or institution attempting to better manage an ever-changing, diverse, and complex population.

Appendix

APPENDIX 1

Please visit the website http://studentthreatassessment.org to view a collection of the forms and protocols that are used within the Level 1 process of the student threat assessment system. Each is written with identification information specific to Salem-Keizer Public Schools; however, each form can easily bc adapted as an example or a template for other districts or agencies to implement. They are referenced as:

1 A. Systems Flow Chart
1 B. Level 1 Assessment Protocol
1 B.1. Level 1 Assessment Protocol, Simplified
1 B.2. Level 1 Assessment, Short-Form
1 C. Guide
1 D. Teacher Questionnaire
1 E. Parent Questionnaire
1 F. Companion to Level 1 Protocol
1 G. Notification Log
1 H. Notification Letter
1 I.   Plan to Protect Targeted Student

APPENDIX 2

Additionally at http://studentthreatassessment.org is a collection of the forms and protocols that are used within the Level 2 process of the student threat assessment system. Each is written with identification information specific to Salem-Keizer Public Schools, Marion County law enforcement agencies, and the Marion County Mental Health Department; however, each form can easily be adapted as an example or a template for other districts or agencies to implement. They are referenced as:

2 A. Level 2 Screening Questions
2 B. Level 2 Summary
2 C. Student Interview
2 D. Level 2 Investigation Protocol (education)
2 E. Risk Rubric
2 F. Resource Menu (Level 2)
2 G. Mental Health Level 2 Protocol
2 H. Law Enforcement Level 2 Protocol
2 I.   At-a-Glance Summary
2 J.   STAT Reference and Review (information glossary)
2 K. Memorandum of Understanding

Glossary of Terms

Rod Swinehart, John Van Dreal, Martin Speckmaier

504: Federal law requiring modifications for people with disabilities to access public agencies.

Accelerators: Those destabilizing factors that increase the potential for individuals to resort to violence. These include illness, divorce, death of a loved one, financial crisis, termination of employment, perceived abandonment/rejection.

ADA: Americans with Disabilities Act.

ADD: Attention deficit disorder.

Adjudication: This term is used for juveniles when the court finds them responsible for a crime, takes jurisdiction, and places them on probation. Note: The adult equivalent would be "conviction." The term *conviction* is not used with juveniles, unless it is a Measure 11 (Oregon Law).

Affective Aggression: Aggression or the threat of aggression while presenting an affectation of high arousal, anger, threats, rage, and bravado. The attacker acts in an emotional or highly aroused state in response to perceived challenge, threat, insult, other affront, or to intimidate and scare. While those engaged in targeted violence may affect rage and bravado, most affective aggression is a reaction or defense, but without premeditation, planning, plotting, or specific targeting.

Aggression Continuum: Eric Johnson's (2000) continuum of aggressive behavior ranging from high-frequency but low-impact behaviors such as pushing, slapping, or kicking to low-frequency but high-impact behaviors such as stabbing, shooting, and so on. Johnson defines behavior that does not cause serious or lethal injury as "aggression," while he defines behavior that causes serious or lethal injury as "extreme aggression" or "violence."

Approach Behavior: Includes not only behaviors that bring the perpetrator within proximity to the target, but also those defined as rehearsals to the act:

purchasing a weapon, practicing with the weapon, driving by the victim's home, attending meetings or functions where the target is known to be. See also *Rehearsal*.

ASD: Autism spectrum disorder (special education identification).

Asperger's Syndrome: An autism spectrum disorder. Some suggest a high-functioning form of autism (although there is disagreement on this among clinicians). It is also considered a pervasive development disorder.

ATAP: Acronym for the Association of Threat Assessment Professionals.

Attack-Related Behavior: Behavior that supports the threat as something that is being seriously considered or planned or otherwise suggests that the attacker is engaged in activity that facilitates the execution of the threat.

CDS: Child development specialist.

Clery Act: The Jeanne Clery Disclosure of Campus Security Policy and Campus Crime Statistics Act (1990). Reference to a freshman student at Lehigh University, Pennsylvania, who was raped and murdered in her on-campus dormitory. Her killer was another Lehigh University student. Among other mandates, the act states that college campus administrators have a duty to warn and a duty to protect their students from crime.

Conditional Threat: A threat of harm or misfortune that will occur if another action is not taken or activity completed. The harm is conditional: "If you do not do__I will do__to you" (de Becker, 1998; Calhoun, 1998). A conditional threat can be either direct or veiled. "If you don't cancel graduation, people will get hurt."

CST: Community surveillance team (Juvenile Department).

DD: Developmental disabilities.

DHS: Department of Human Services, previously known as SCF or Services to Children and Families.

Dietz 10: Park Dietz's (reference unobtainable) research produced ten factors that virtually all attackers of public figures have in common.

Direct Threat: A threat characterized by specifics noting intent to do harm and identifying both the victim and the perpetrator. Direct threats are clear and explicit (Calhoun, 1998). "On Monday, I'm going to bring a gun and shoot everyone at school."

DV: Domestic violence.

ED: Emotionally disturbed (special education identification).

Enmeshments: Those things that continue to cause contacts between estranged domestic partners. These include children, shared relationships, or shared ownership of property.

Erotomania: A stalking typology characterized by mental illness. Stalker believes that the victim loves them despite there being no basis in reality for this belief.

Evaluation: Used to indicate a mental health evaluation or psychological evaluation. Addresses the mental health, psychological issues, as well as the behavioral issues of an individual.

Expressive Threat: A threat that is based on emotion and often made an expression of anger, rage, or hatred or as a defense against fear or shame (Meloy, 1988). They can be recognized by their affective nature (i.e., "blowing off steam"); "I could kill you!"

False Victimization: A false report of a crime or other incident such that the actions taken as a result of the report will benefit the reporter. Characterized by attention seeking.

FAPA: Acronym for Family Abuse Prevention Act (federal legislation on restraining orders). Used as a euphemism for a restraining order (also see *Restraining Order*).

FERPA: Family Education Rights and Privacy Act.

HB3444 (3444): 1999 ORS 339.325—ORS 339.327: Major Oregon legislation, which mandated duties and actions of schools around threats and violence.

Hunter/Howler: Hunters are individuals who are engaged in serious targeted violence. Hunters do not draw unnecessary attention to themselves by making threats, as their intention is to complete their violent plan. Howlers are individuals who make repeated threats to harm. These threats may be made in a variety of forms: written, phone, or through a third party. Howlers do not engage in approach behavior, as they have no real intent to carry out their threats. Howlers don't hunt and hunters don't howl. From Dr. Fredrick Calhoun, *Hunters and Howlers*, USMS Publication, 1998.

IDEA: Individuals with Disabilities Education Act.

IEP: Individual education plan.

Incarceration: Adults and/or parents that are in jail or prison.

Indirect Threat: A threat is present but is ambiguous or otherwise unclear. The threat may be tentative with masked or evasive references to victim, perpetrator, plan, and justification, but the violence is definitely implied (O'Toole, 2000). "I have what I need to kill everyone in this class."

Inhibitors: Those stabilizing factors that reduce the potential for individuals to resort to violence. These include religious beliefs, friends, family, employment, hobbies, pride, and dignity.

Instrumental Threat: A threat made to control or influence the target's behavior (Meloy, 1988). They can be recognized by their conditional nature: "If you ____, then I'll ____!"

Intervention: An action taken to decrease or stop violence potential.

Intuition: Any quick insight, recognized immediately without a reasoning process; a belief arrived at unconsciously; often it is based on extensive experience of a subject.

JACA: Acronym for Justification, no Alternatives, accepts Consequences, and has Ability (de Becker, 1998).

LD: Learning disabled.

LEUR: Law enforcement unit record. A record that may contain suicide risk assessments, restraining orders, and other documentation that is not considered part of the education record. The LEUR may be accessed by school administrators, counselors, law enforcement, or other members of the law enforcement unit.

Level 1 Screening: Threat assessment/screening done by a school site team consisting of an administrator, counselor/CDS, an SRO, a teacher who knows the student, and others as appropriate (parent, case manager if special education or 504, etc.).

Level 2 Assessment: Threat assessment done through the combined efforts of STAT and school site team. Available if school site team determines, after conducting a Level 1 assessment, that the case needs further investigation, assessment, and supervision.

Liaison Officer: Also referred to as SRO, school resource officer.

Love Obsessional Stalking: A stalking typology characterized by mental illness. The stalker is obsessed with love for the victim despite there being no relationship or previous relationship on which to base this emotion.

MDT: Multidisciplinary team.

Measure 11 (Oregon): Mandatory minimum sentencing crime.

Meloy Triad: Methamphetamine, firearms, paranoia. Reid Meloy concludes that given the presence of any two of these, one can relatively safely assume the presence of the third.

Menninger Triad: A wish to die, a wish to kill, a wish to be killed (suicidal, homicidal, suicide by cop). Karl Menninger concluded the high probability of a poor outcome when these three desires are present.

Mosaic: A computer-assisted assessment tool developed by Gavin de Becker. There are a number of variations of this tool, depending on the type of situation being assessed: school violence, domestic violence, threats to public officials, abortion clinics, workplace violence, stalking.

MOU: Memorandum of understanding.

MRDD: Mentally retarded/developmentally disabled.

PDD: Pervasive developmental disorder, characterized by abnormal social interaction and communication deficits.

Preincident Indicators: Actions, communications, or circumstances that indicate an individual or group is considering or planning a violent act.

Protective Response: Initiated through risk management. An investigation and plan that addresses the physical vulnerability of a school, classroom, students, and/or staff members. Used when a target has been identified through a threat.

Pucker Factor: A sensation experienced by law enforcement officers, elevating their concerns and amplifying their vigilance.

RAD: Reactive attachment disorder.

Reactive Aggression (Impulsive) (Impromptu): Unplanned aggression resulting from an imminent threat, insult, or affront, either real or perceived. Characterized by the emotions of fear or anger with the goal of eliminating the threat and gaining or maintaining control. While the aggression may be unplanned, the perpetrator may have been preemptively prepared to become aggressive if challenged. Often a matter of poor socialization or coping strategies. Is sometimes referred to as affective aggression (see *Affective Aggression*).

Rehearsal: Actions of an individual that mimic practice or otherwise prepare for a targeted act of violence. Examples might include practicing with a weapon, ritualistic cleaning of firearms, or in some way acting out parts of a premeditated plan of violence.

Release Agreement: A written promise an arrestee agrees to upon release from custody pending trial on criminal charges. Also referred to as recognizance when the agreement is between the arrestee (defendant) and the court. Release agreements have general conditions such as a promise to appear in court as required and may contain special conditions limiting the defendant's contacts, movements, and behaviors.

RO: Restraining order. The acronym TRO is also sometimes used (temporary restraining order). (See also *FAPA*.)

Sadistic Stalker: A stalking typology characterized by a desire to punish, harm, or terrorize. Simple obsessional stalkers can reach this level of hatred and anger.

Simple Obsessional Stalking: A stalking typology characterized by a refusal to accept rejection. The majority of stalking cases that result from a failed relationship fall within this typology.

SRO: School resource officer. Also referred to as liaison officer.

STAT: Mid-Valley Student Threat Assessment Team. Members include Salem-Keizer School District, Marion County Sheriff's Department, Salem Police Department, Keizer Police Department, Marion County Court Security, Marion and Polk County Juvenile Departments, Oregon Youth Authority, Marion and Polk County Mental Health Departments, and Willamette Education Service District. The team conducts Level 2 assessment, assists with threat management strategies, and explores resources.

Supervision Plan: A documented plan of modifications, interventions, and measures taken to reduce problems and circumstances that trigger, precipitate, or aggravate a dangerous situation. The supervision plan may also address long-term interventions.

Tarasoff (Tarasoff Warning / Tarasoff Principle): Reference to a University of California student who was stalked and killed by fellow student Prosenjit Poddar after he had discussed his intention to kill her with a University Health Service psychologist. Her family sued, and the resulting court opinions formed the basis for general acceptance of the notion that treating professionals have a duty to protect known intended victims (Tarasoff v. Regents, 17 Cal. 3d 425, 551 P.2d 334, 131 Cal. Rptr. 14 (1976).

Target: An individual, group, or property identified as the focus of harm or damage in a threatening or dangerous situation.

Targeted Violence: Any incident of violence where a known or knowable attacker selects a particular target prior to their violent attack. Behavior is planned, plotted, and premeditated. Frequently not in feature of explosive emotional reaction. Is frequently characterized by minimal or no emotion with a variety of goals such as power, revenge, dominance, money, or sexual gratification. May also be accompanied with rage; however, the rage is an affectation used to intimidate or for theatrical effect, but is likely not a feature of an emotional outburst.

TAT: Acronym for the Marion County Adult Threat Advisement Team.

Threat Assessment: The investigation of a threat made by an individual or group as well as an examination, survey, and consideration of the behavior patterns, conditions, circumstances, and variables of danger in or surrounding an individual or group.

Trigger: An experience or circumstance that aggravates an individual or group further toward a violent act.

Triggering Event: The proverbial "straw that broke the camel's back." This might include the loss of a significant inhibitor or the introduction of a major accelerator in a person's life. This event may be viewed by outsiders as insignificant; however, to the principal this event causes the loss of alternatives or intolerable outcomes.

Veiled Threat: A threat that implies violence but does not clearly threaten it. The threat may be characterized by specifics but vague in one of two ways: either uncertainty about who will carry out the threat or uncertainty about who will be the victim (de Becker, 1998; Calhoun, 1998). "You may not want to come to school on Tuesday; something terrible may happen."

Violence Continuum: U.S. Secret Service's Exceptional Case Studies Project (Dr. Robert Fein, Special Agent Bryan Vossekuil, and Special Agent John Berglund) found that lethal and near-lethal attackers of public figures followed a recognizable and identifiable pattern of behavior. In a subsequent study of school shootings (1992) this continuum was also present. This pattern is ideation, planning, preparation, and execution.

YST: Youth Services Team.

References, Additional Readings, and Resources

PAPERS AND ARTICLES

"A Potential for Violent Injury." *Oregon Health Trends*. Series 56, June 2000.

Borum, R., Fein, R., Vossekuil, B., Berglund, J. "Threat Assessment; Defining an Approach for Evaluating Risk of Targeted Violence." *Behavioral Sciences and the Law*, 1999, 17(3): 323–337.

Cornell, D., Sherss, P., Kaplan, S., et al. "Guidelines for Student Threat Assessment; Field-Test Findings." *School Psych Review*, 2004, 33(4): 527–546.

Courtwright, D. "Violence in America." *American Heritage*, Sept. 1996: 37–51.

Drysdale, D., Modzeleski, W., and Simons, A. *Campus Attacks: Targeted Violence Affecting Institutions of Higher Education*. U.S. Secret Service, U.S. Department of Homeland Security, Office of Safe and Drug-Free Schools, U.S. Department of Education, and Federal Bureau of Investigation, U.S. Department of Justice. Washington, D.C., 2010.

Dwyer, K., Osher, D., and Warger, C. *Early Warning, Timely Response: A Guide to Safe Schools*. Washington, D.C.: U.S. Department of Education. 1998.

Fein, R., and Vossekuil, B. *Protective Intelligence and Threat Assessment Investigations*. U.S. Department of Justice. 1998.

Fein, R., Vossekuil, B., and Holden, G. *Threat Assessment: An Approach to Prevent Targeted Violence*. U.S. Department of Justice. 1995.

Fein, R., Vossekuil, B., Pollack, W., Borum, R., Modzeleski, W., Reddy, M. *Threat Assessment in Schools: A Guide to Managing Threatening Situations and to Creating Safe School Climates*. U.S. Secret Service National Threat Assessment Center, U.S. Department of Education, National Institute of Justice. 2002.

Forth, A., Kosson, D., and Hare, R. D. *Psychopathy Checklist: Youth Version*. Toronto, Mental Health: Health System. 1996.

Frick, P., O'Brien, B., Wooten, J., and McBurnett, K. "Psychopathy and Conduct Problems in Children." *Journal of Abnormal Psychology*, 103, 4, 700–707. 1994.

Gelles, M., Sasaki-Swindle, K., Palarea, R. "Threat Assessment: A Partnership between Law Enforcement and Mental Health." *Journal of Threat Assessment*, 2(1) 55–66. 2002.

Grossman, D. *Teaching Kids to Kill: Classical Conditioning.* Killology Research Group. 2000.

Grossman. D. *Trained to Kill: Are We Conditioning Our Children to Commit Murder?* Killology Research Group. 2001.

Jenkins, P. "Mommy's Little Monster: Does the Family Breed Serial Killers?" *Chronicles*, 21–23. May 1999.

Johnson, E. *Advanced Topics in the Assessment of Youth Violence.* Oregon Forensic Institute. 2000.

Kelling, G., Wilson, J. "Broken Windows." *The Atlantic.* March 1982.

Lynam, D. "Early Identification of Chronic Offenders: Who Is the Fledgling Psychopath?" *Psychological Bulletin*, 120(2), 209–234, 1996.

Meloy, J. R. "The Empirical Basis and Forensic Application of Affective and Predatory Violence." *Australian and New Zealand J of Psychiatry*, 40, 539–547. 2006.

Oberlander, L. *Responding to Children and Youths Who Threaten Violence.* University of Massachusetts.

O'Toole, M. *The School Shooter: A Threat Assessment Perspective.* Federal Bureau of Investigation, Department of Justice. 2000.

Podles, L. "The Vital Tradition of Manhood." *The American Enterprise*, March/April, 25–26. 1997.

Project MEGIDDO. Federal Bureau of Investigation. Department of Justice.

Pynchon, M. R., and Borum, R. "Assessing Threats of Targeted Group Violence: Contribution from Social Psychology." *Behavioral Sciences and the Law* 17: 339–355. 1999.

Reddy, M., Borum, R., Berlund, J., Vossekuil, B., Fein, R., and Modzeleski, W. "Evaluating Risk for Targeted Violence in Schools: Comparing Risk Assessment, Threat Assessment, and Other Approaches." John Wiley & Sons, Inc. *Psychology in the Schools*, 38(2), 2001.

Reducing School Violence: Building a Framework for School Safety. Southeastern Regional Vision for Education and the Florida Department of Education with assistance from the Southeast Regional Center for Drug-Free Schools and Communities.

Smith, S. "From Violent Words to Violent Deeds." *The International Journal of Speech, Language and the Law.* Vol. 15.1, 105–107. 2008.

Student Profiling. Center for the Study and Prevention of Violence. Position paper #5. PS 004, 2000.

"U.S. Proposes New Rules on Student Privacy." *Inside Higher Ed.* March 24, 2008.

Van Dreal, J., Cunningham, M., Nishioka, V. *Mid-Valley Student Threat Assessment System: Making Schools Safer through a Multi-Agency Collaboration.* Hamilton Fish Institute, Persistently Safe Schools 2005, paper #9505, 249–258.

Vellinden, S., Hersen, M., and Thomas, J. *Risk Factors in School Shootings.* Pacific University, Forest Grove, Oregon.

"Violence: A Neglected Mode of Behavior." *Annals of the American Academy of Political and Social Science* 364, 50–59. 1966.

Vossekuil, B., Fein, R., Reddy, M., Borum, R., Modzeleski, W. *The Final Report and Findings of the Safe School Initiative: Implications for the Prevention of School At-*

tacks in the United States. U.S. Secret Service National Threat Assessment Center, U.S. Department of Education, National Institute of Justice, 2002.

Vossekuil, B., Reddy, M., and Fein, R. *An Interim Report on the Prevention of Targeted Violence in Schools.* U.S. Secret Service National Threat Assessment Center, U.S. Department of Education, National Institute of Justice, 2000.

Walker, H., Irvin, C., Sprague, J. *Violence Prevention and School Safety: Issues, Problems, Approaches and Recommended Solutions.* University of Oregon, 1997.

Books

Borum, R., Bartel, P., Forth, A. *Manual for the Structured Assessment of Violence Risk in Youth (SAVRY).* University of South Florida. 2002.

Calhoun, F. *Hunters and Howlers: Threats and Violence against Federal Judicial Officials in the United States Virginia.* FBI. 1998.

Corcoran, M., and Cawood, J. *Violence Assessment and Intervention: The Practitioner's Handbook.* CRC Press, 2003.

de Becker, Gavin. *The Gift of Fear: Survival Signals That Protect Us from Violence.* New York: Little, Brown and Company, 1998.

de Becker, Gavin. *Protecting the Gift of Fear: Keeping Children and Teenagers Safe (and Parents Sane).* New York: Little, Brown and Company, 1999.

Grossman, D., and DeGaetano, G. *Stop Teaching Our Kids to Kill: A Call to Action Against TV, Movie and Video Game Violence.* Random House, 1999.

Loeber, R., and Farrington, D. *Serious and Violent Juvenile Offenders: Risk Factors and Successful Interventions.* California: Sage Publications, 1998.

Meloy, J. R. *The Psychopathic Mind.* Northvale, N.J.: Aronson, 1988.

Meloy, J. R. *Violence Risk and Threat Assessment: A Practical Guide for Mental Health and Criminal Justice Professionals.* San Diego: Specialized Training Services, 2000.

Mohandie, K. *School Violence Threat Management.* Specialized Training Services, San Diego, California, 2000.

Newman, K. *Rampage: The Social Roots of School Shootings.* Basic Books, 2004.

United States Secret Services and United States Department of Education/Fein et al. *The Final Report and Findings of the Safe School Initiative: Implications for the Prevention of School Attacks in the United States.* Washington, D.C., May 2002.

United States Secret Services and United States Department of Education/Fein et al. *Threat Assessment in Schools.* Washington, D.C., May 2002.

Resources

Association of Threat Assessment Professionals
1215 K Street #2290
Sacramento, CA 95814
916-231-2146

Crisis Management Institute
www.cmionline.org
Salem, OR
503-585-3484

Eric M. Johnson, Ph.D., ABPP
Oregon Forensic Institute
1942 NW Kearney, Suite 21
Portland, OR 97209
503-274-4017

Factor One
P.O. Box 1772
San Leandro, CA 94577
510-352-8660

Gavin de Becker and Associates
11684 Ventura Blvd., Suite 440
Studio City, CA 91604

National Center for the Analysis of Violent Crime
FBI Academy
Quantico, VA 22135

The Safe School Initiative
Final Findings
Education Publications Center
U.S. Department of Education
P.O. Box 1398
Jessup, MD 20794
877-433-7827

Specialized Training Services
P.O. Box 28181
San Diego, CA 92198
800-848-1226

About the Authors

Raymond Byrd is the security manager for Salem-Keizer Public Schools. He has twenty-six years of law enforcement and security experience, including work as a school resource officer, a detective, arson investigator, background investigator, and a police corporal. As security manager, he supervises thirty security staff and administers all aspects of the school district's physical security and the contractual relationships with local law enforcement and private security. He is a member of both Oregon's Marion County Adult Threat Advisory Team and the Mid-Valley Student Threat Assessment Team. He works daily with educators, law enforcement, and trial court personnel in the assessment and management of adult threats of aggression within the school district, and he consults regularly with school districts throughout Oregon and Washington. Raymond is a member of the Association of Threat Assessment Professionals.

Seth Elliott is a behavior consultant and crisis intervention trainer with the Salem-Keizer School District. He is also a certified Krav Maga instructor and an executive protection specialist. He teaches and speaks on effective communication, stress management, conflict resolution, and cultural issues related to aggression. He is a member of Oregon's Mid-Valley Student Threat Assessment Team and the Marion County Threat Advisory Team. He works daily designing behavioral programs for students in situations ranging from mild to extremely aggressive behavior. Seth is a member of the Association of Threat Assessment Professionals.

Darling Mendoza has been working through the Victim Assistance Division of the Marion County District Attorney's Office since 2003. Prior to working with the DA's office, she was employed by Catholic Charities' culturally specific El Program Hispano as a long-term case manager, where she assisted Hispanic families in escaping abusive situations and achieving self-sufficiency through Housing for Urban Development (HUD) funding. She is a member of Oregon's Marion County Threat Advisory Team and a consultant to the Mid-Valley Student Threat Assessment Team, where she provides frequent counsel on safety planning for victims of aggressive crimes and abuse.

Dave Okada began his law enforcement career in 1987 and is a lieutenant with the Salem Police Department. He is a member of Oregon's Marion County Adult Threat Advisory Team and the Mid-Valley Student Threat Assessment Team and coordinates departmental participation and investigations on both teams. He is a current member of FBI Joint Terrorist Task Force, a member of the local FBI Terrorism Working Group, and actively participates in the criminal intelligence network in the Salem area. He works daily as a practitioner in threat assessment and has been instrumental in the promotion of threat assessment teams throughout the Northwest region. He has been a member of the Association of Threat Assessment Professionals since 2003 and is currently serving as association's Northwest Chapter president.

Allan Rainwater is a mental health practitioner with Marion County Health Department and has twenty-five years of experience working within the fields of crisis intervention and counseling. He has been instrumental in maintaining the presence of a public mental health perspective within the threat assessment system and conducts threat assessments on a regular basis. He consults at every level of the system, especially regarding resources and diagnostic interpretation. He trains and consults with mental health practitioners throughout the Northwest Region and is a member of Oregon's Mid-Valley Student Threat Assessment Team and the Marion County Threat Advisory Team. He is a member of the Association of Threat Assessment Professionals.

Shelley Spady is a licensed clinical social worker and a professional school counselor who has provided clinical and other supportive services to children, adolescents, and families in both education and psychiatric settings since 1997. She is currently a family support advocate and is the threat assessment team leader for the Willamette Education Service District, serving rural schools in Oregon's Marion, Polk, and Yamhill Counties. She is a member of the Association of Threat Assessment Professionals and sits as a member of the Mid-Valley Student Threat Assessment Team, the Yamhill County Student Threat Assessment Team, and the Marion County Threat Advisory Team.

Martin Speckmaier is the owner of Comprehensive School and Workplace Safety, LLC. He provides consultations, presentations, and trainings to school campuses and communities, addresses the latest campus-specific safety issues, and provides strategies to keep schools safe. He has twenty-three years of law enforcement experience as a patrol officer, narcotics detective, sexual assault detective, and campus resource liaison officer. He has trained and implemented effective and sustainable student threat assessment teams in many school districts and Education Service Districts throughout Washington State and the Pacific Northwest. He was lead trainer and consultant in the establishing of Washington State's first county-wide student threat assessment team, unifying seven school districts, nine law enforcement agencies, the county mental health provider, and various community stakeholders with protective responsibilities. His work and investigations have been showcased in *America's Most Wanted, Reader's Digest* magazine, FOX News, and numerous local and national news stations. Martin is a member of the Association of Threat Assessment Professionals.

Rod Swinehart has over thirty years of experience in a variety of criminal justice capacities, with the majority of this experience being the assessment of individuals, departments, and organizations regarding issues of security and efficiency. He has personally conducted over ten thousand interviews with criminal defendants, their families, friends, and their alleged victims. Rod coordinated the formation of Oregon's Marion County Threat Advisory Team in 1999 and currently serves as its chairman. In 2005, he received an award of recognition from the Northwest Chapter of the Association of Threat Assessment Professionals for his contributions to the practice of threat assessment. Rod currently serves as the vice president of the Northwest Chapter of the Association of Threat Assessment Professionals and as president of Protective Research, Inc., primarily providing safety and security consultation to school districts in the mid-valley and training to districts and agencies throughout the Northwest.

John Van Dreal is a school psychologist with the Salem-Keizer School District and has over two decades of experience in psychoeducational evaluation, crisis assessment and intervention, behavioral intervention, and systems design. In 1999, he began the development and implementation of the multiagency student threat assessment system reviewed within this book. Through that collaboration, he has worked daily with educators, law enforcement, trial-court personnel, juvenile justice, and mental health personnel in the assessment and management of threats of aggression within the schools and the community. He is Chair of Oregon's Mid-Valley Student Threat Assessment

Team and is a member of the Marion County Threat Advisory Team. He is a member of the Association of Threat Assessment Professionals and regularly provides training and consultation on student threat assessment systems and youth violence to regional and national audiences.